THE REFERENCE SHELF   VOLUME 42 NUMBER 1

PROTECTING OUR ENVIRONMENT

EDITED BY

GRANT S. McCLELLAN

Editor, Current Magazine

THE H. W. WILSON COMPANY
NEW YORK   1970

THE REFERENCE SHELF

The books in this series contain reprints of articles, excerpts from books, and addresses on current issues and social trends in the United States and other countries. There are six separately bound numbers in each volume, all of which are generally published in the same calendar year. One number is a collection of recent speeches; each of the others is devoted to a single subject and gives background information and discussion from various points of view, concluding with a comprehensive bibliography.

Subscribers to the current volume receive the books as issued. The subscription rate is $17 in the United States and Canada ($20 foreign) for a volume of six numbers. Single numbers are $4 each in the United States and Canada ($4.50 foreign).

PROTECTING OUR ENVIRONMENT

Copyright © 1970
By The H. W. Wilson Company

International Standard Book Number 0-8242-0409-3

Library of Congress Catalog Card Number 72-95636

PREFACE

Protecting our natural environment has become a crucial national, even planetary, issue. The recognition of the complex problems involved in the deterioration of our environment has come about quickly, though at a late date. Scarcely more than a decade or so ago only conservationists were voicing alarm. Now some of our most eminent scientists predict mankind itself is endangered unless corrective action is taken, and taken soon.

At the core of the problem are man's population explosion and his ever-expanding technological advances. Both make heavy drains on the earth's resources and the atmosphere surrounding the globe. And both increasingly cause serious damage to the natural habitat.

As note has been taken of these developments, the science of ecology—the study of the total interrelations of the natural processes of growth and decay in nature and man's role in those processes—claims increasing public attention. We are coming to understand, now more quickly perhaps with man's exploits in space, that indeed the earth is but a spaceship itself. And we are its custodians.

These striking and fundamental concepts underlie much of the current thinking about our environmental resources and their protection. The various sections of this compilation also reflect this new approach. Thus, in the first section several selections deal with the global aspects of pollution problems. The middle sections, though dealing more specifically with American environmental issues—air pollution, rescuing our waterways, and dealing with our natural landscape—also relate to global issues. The last section, concerned with the national measures now being taken on environmental issues, also turns at the end to foreign and international attempts to protect the environment.

3

Now, most fortunately, the youth of our nation and of
other countries have become seriously concerned about the
environment in which we live. In the spring of 1970 this will
become publicly evident when college and high school students and other community groups will participate in a national environmental "teach-in" or "E-Day" (for Environment Day or Earth Day). The proposal was first sparked by
Senator Gaylord Nelson (Democrat, Wisconsin) as an effort
not only to educate citizens but to stress ways in which all
citizens can help in halting pollution.

The editor wishes to thank the authors and the publish-
ers of the selections which follow for permission to reprint
them in this compilation.

Grant S. McClellan

January 1970

A NOTE TO THE READER

The reader's attention is directed to an earlier Reference
Shelf compilation which deals with one aspect of the pollution problem: *The Water Crisis* (Volume 38, Number 6),
edited by George A. Nikolaieff and published in 1967.

CONTENTS

I. OUR ENDANGERED PLANET

EDITOR'S INTRODUCTION

Global aspects of our environmental problems are dealt with in this opening section. The first article, by David Perlman, drawn from *Look* Magazine, deals with this question and indicates that the mass media are well aware of the dangers we confront.

Just how serious those dangers are can be gathered from the next article, in which a writer on scientific problems deals with environmental problems that have arisen in the short period since man gained control of atomic power.

The section closes with an overall look at America's environmental dangers by Gaylord A. Nelson, former Governor of and now Democratic Senator from Wisconsin, who is one of our national political leaders most concerned with pollution and related issues.

POLLUTING OUR PLANET [1]

This year [1969] America took a firsthand look at the moon. But in years to come, 1969 may best be remembered as the year of our first long view of America the Beautiful and the rest of our earth. The Apollo capsules, invisible in the vastness of space, broadcasting television images back to American viewers, became mirrors in which we could see ourselves anew. It was a humbling experience.

From Apollo, the receding earth looked as lonely in space as the spacecraft seemed from earth. Suddenly, we could understand what Adlai Stevenson had said:

We travel together, passengers on a little spaceship; dependent on its vulnerable reserves of air and soil; all committed for

[1] Reprint of "America the Beautiful?" by David Perlman, journalist and free-lance writer. *Look*. 33:25-7. N. 4, '69. By permission of the editors. From the November 4, 1969 issue of *Look* Magazine. Copyright 1969 by Cowles Communications, Inc.

our safety to its security and peace; preserved from annihilation only by the care, the work and . . . the love we give our fragile craft.

The earth was revealed as Apollo's twin: Spaceship Earth. Man on one spaceship radioed to man on the other: "The earth from here is a grand oasis in the . . . vastness of space!" An oasis: a fragile outpost of life in a lifeless pocket of the universe. But the astronauts, sustained by their intricate, perfectly functioning man-made life systems, could see signs of trouble in the more complex, natural life systems of Spaceship Earth.

The Apollo 10 astronauts, looking down on America the Beautiful, easily picked out Los Angeles. Even from orbit, they recognized its sink of whiskey-brown smog, where 4 million cars vomit unburned hydrocarbons, tetraethyl lead and cancer-causing nickel additives; where 16 million rubber tires vaporize on the abrading freeways and invisible but deadly asbestos particles shed from brake linings.

In orbit, the astronauts passed over other trouble spots, spreading cancerlike in the "oasis" of earth below. Everywhere are the works of modern man, yet all his technology—products of the same genius that created the spaceship's perfect environment—has neither created a fit environment for the human community nor preserved the precious diversity and plenty of the other organisms with which man shares this planet.

Indeed, the impact of technology on the earth's ecology—the indivisible web of life—threatens the continued existence of life itself. The life-support system of Spaceship Earth is no less fragile than that of Apollo. Applied without wisdom or prudence, the same technology that is our servant may prove to be our ultimate executioner. This Jekyll-to-Hyde switch is most evident in America, the citadel of modern technology, but the same phenomenon has been spreading all around the world, keeping step with what we self-deceptively call progress.

The Impact of Technology

Off Bermuda, a rocky islet stands in the Atlantic. It harbors one hundred sea-feeding petrels, birds that never touch a continental land mass. A gentle dust, windblown from North African croplands three thousand miles away, falls to the ocean and poisons fish with DDT from the dust motes. The Bermuda petrels, last of their species, feed on the fish and lay eggs that never hatch. Extinction is near for the petrel. Other species face the same fate.

Eastward across the Atlantic, the Algerian Sahara is spotted with the ragged green of date-palm groves. Two thousand wells lower underground water levels, and a million date palms die. The sands advance, threatening the livelihood of 120,000 desert dwellers.

Eastward still, the sands and salt marshes of Southern Iraq reveal how long men have plundered this planet. Ur of the Chaldees towered here above all other cities in the days of Abraham; but the exploited earth struck back, dams and canals silted up. For two thousand years, the land of Ur has been almost as dead as the moon.

Vast India, a nation only twenty years old, takes seven minutes to cross by satellite. Its troubles scar the land with a havoc of numbers: eight sprawling cities with up to 5 million underfed humans in each; a bursting population of 550 million that grows by 12 to 13 million a year, while valiant but futile family-planning campaigns touch 3 to 4 million at best.

Beyond Asia, the blue of oceans seems unmarred for seven thousand miles. Yet on islands below, phosphate mining, bomb testing and lagoon draining have destroyed fragile ecosystems and driven away whole communities of men and animals. In the creatures of the sea, new man-made chemicals, like a time bomb, are working their way through nucleus and fat body, oviduct and bloodstream, ready for a reckoning.

In Egypt, the great mainstream of the Nile river, its mouths emptying into the Mediterranean, is now controlled by the Aswan High Dam, more than six hundred miles upstream from the sea. Three miles across, the massive dam impounds a lake three hundred miles long, and growing. Dr. Mohammed Abdul-Fattah al Kassas of the University of Cairo tells how Aswan has slowed the Nile's downstream flow so that protective dunes and sandbars no longer build up along the delta shore to fend off the invading sea. The Mediterranean is flooding in on the delta, and one million acres of fertile farmlands are disappearing under salt water. The village where Dr. al Kassas was born is now buried beneath the sea, two miles out from the delta's new shoreline. And on the surface of vast Lake Nasser, above the Aswan dam, wild water hyacinths that evaporate water into the air are spreading. The lake may lose as much water by evaporation each year as it is supposed to send down the Nile for irrigation. But poisoning the hyacinths would mean poisoning the lake.

Dr. Henry van der Schalie, University of Michigan zoologist and veteran disease fighter in Egypt's villages, predicts that snails carrying the wormlike blood flukes of schistosomiasis will soon infest five hundred miles of new irrigation canals below Aswan. Peasants irrigating land from these new canals, he says, will succumb to the painful and virtually incurable disease.

Aswan is already a liability for Egypt's fishermen, according to Dr. Carl J. George of Union College. The flooding Nile used to carry 50 to 100 million tons of nutrient-rich sediments a year out to sea, but the nutrients no longer flow, and the fish catch has collapsed. The economic loss is $7 million a year, and Egyptian fishing families have abandoned their rake-sailed feluccas for the indifferent slums of Alexandria and Cairo.

Aswan is a bitter example of "ecological backlash," in the phrase of Dr. Barry Commoner of Washington University. Other so-called technological triumphs are setting off a backlash all over the world. In Santa Barbara, for example, the Union Oil Company's new offshore well has spilled some 3.5 million gallons of crude petroleum into the sea since last January [1969] when drilling operations created a leak in the undersea rock structure. Until that geological formation empties, oil will continue to push up through ancient earthquake fissures, even if it's pumped, and the beaches and birds of the Santa Barbara channel will be threatened. It may last twenty years. Already, entire populations of seabirds—cormorants, grebes and mergansers—have been destroyed by the upwelling oil. Kelp beds have suffocated, and tidal plankton has been killed. Clinging to particles of sediment, tons of oil have sunk. No one knows what damage is done to fragile species of sea-bottom organisms with which the whole cycle of oceanic life is linked.

Aquatic life suffers from too much heat—thermal pollution—as well as from oil. Most power plants—nuclear or conventional—burn fuel to heat water to turn turbines to generate electricity. Hot waste water is dumped into streams and oceans; many fish die under a temperature rise of only a few degrees, and the aquatic ecosystem shifts abruptly.

Land and water can die from other ecological time bombs. Excess fertilizers standing on farm fields sterilize the soil; runoff pollutes waterways with nitrates. Phosphates have overnourished Lake Erie to death. Two thousand silt-filled irrigation dams in America stand useless, while upstream banks erode. Strip mining in Missouri, Kentucky, Illinois and West Virginia has left vicious, unhealing scars on the land and damaged thirteen thousand miles of streams through acid drainage. In Hudspeth County, Texas, below El Paso on the Rio Grande, secondhand irrigation water is so salty the Federal Land Bank sells abandoned farms, once valued at $1,000 an acre, for $50 an acre.

Life's Fundamental "Food Chain"

If these were isolated instances of technological error, they could be written off as the price of progress, regrettable but unavoidable. But as human population increases and technology improves, man in his ecological blindness is suicidally attacking the foundation of life itself.

Look for a moment at a concept basic to ecology—the "food chain." It is an intricate chain, beginning in the seas, where the evolution of all organisms, including man, began. Throughout the oceans of the world drift immense, uncountable masses of microscopic plants known as phytoplankton. These plants carry out the most important biological process on our planet, the process called photosynthesis, by which sunlight and carbon dioxide are transformed into oxygen and carbohydrates. Without phytoplankton, there would be no air to breathe, no life on earth.

Phytoplankton are also the pastures of the ocean, the first organisms in the food chain. Browsing on those pastures are the zooplankton—the smallest animal life of the marine world. The great toothless baleen whales—many virtually extinct because of man's indiscriminate hunting—feed directly on plankton; but most of it is eaten by hordes of small fish like anchovies, sardines, herring and the young of larger fish. Huge adult fish, like tuna and sharks, feed on the smaller ones. And into these upper links in the food chain come man and the birds of prey. They both eat the smaller fish; man alone takes the larger ones.

All food chains share a common characteristic: biological concentration. It takes one hundred pounds of grass, digested by a steer, to become one pound of meat; one hundred pounds of meat yield a pound of new human tissue. At sea, the nutrients of phytoplankton are concentrated tenfold in zooplankton, tenfold again in small fish, tenfold in larger ones, tenfold again in humans or seabirds.

And in this almost unimaginably intricate process of concentration lies one of the central dangers of man's ecological carelessness: polluting the food chain in any of its simpler links can destroy the more complex ones.

The most dramatic example of this is the effect of DDT, that long-lasting, powerful pesticide that has saved so many

millions of lives from malaria and typhus and multiplied
the world's crop yields since World War II. Twenty-five years
ago, DDT was chemistry's greatest boon to man. After
twenty-five years, scientists now know DDT takes a decade or
more to lose its potency, that it circulates globally, like fallout, that it vaporizes along with moisture from green fields,
that it kills harmless and beneficial insects along with pests,
and that it concentrates primarily in the fatty tissues of
plants and animals, entering the food chain at the first link—
the seaborne phytoplankton—and building to its highest concentration in the later links, including man.

Antarctic penguins, Bermuda petrels, Lake Michigan
coho salmon, all contain the man-made poison or its toxic
residues. The breast milk of American mothers contains .2
parts per million of DDT, four times the "safe" level the
Federal Government allows in shipment of cows' milk for
human consumption.

Even as it is losing its effectiveness as a pesticide, DDT
is blamed for the extinction of peregrine falcons as a breeding species in the Eastern states, for the failure of California
pelicans to breed along the West Coast this year [1969], for
the death of crab larvae off San Francisco's Golden Gate.

Fortunately, substitutes for DDT are emerging from current research. But these efforts are carried on under relent-
less pressure for more food production faster—pressure that
stems from the growth of world population, particularly in
the hungriest nations. The world now holds nearly 3.5 billion people; we'll have 6 billion before 2001. The President's
Science Advisory Committee, calling recently for aggressive
programs of population control, foresees a major world crisis
of "malnutrition, economic deterioration and political in-
stability" in many nations between now and 1985. Already,
half the world's people, including thousands of Americans,
suffer from undernutrition—not enough to eat; or malnutrition—the wrong kind of food, notably a disease-inducing
lack of protein.

The Biosphere: Our Global Ecosystem

Biologist Barry Commoner, predicting imminent world-wide famine, speaks of the biosphere as man's most important machine:

> This machine is our biological capital, the basic apparatus on which our total productivity depends. If we destroy it, our most advanced technology will come to naught, and any economic and political systems that depend on it will flounder. Yet the major threat to the integrity of this biological capital is technology itself. . . . Technological advances have proved to be powerful intrusions on geophysical and ecological systems. Most of our difficulties result from the failure to recognize this basic fact in time. The failing may become fatal as we progress to the vast new development necessary to avert the impending world famine.

Despite such pleas for an ecological approach to development, huge projects are still planned and executed without adequate study of their effects on the environment.

One of many experiments on the drawing boards is a badly needed new canal at sea level across the Isthmus of Panama. The Atomic Energy Commission is examining the feasibility of blasting out the canal with strings of buried thermonuclear explosives totaling 250 megatons or more in energy yield. This would far exceed the power of all the nuclear bombs ever tested—more force than two or three San Francisco earthquakes. These crater-digging devices would send fallout clouds forty thousand feet high; "short term" radiation hazards would require evacuating tens of thousands of Central American Indians from jungle villages and coastal fishing communities for up to two years. The ecological effects could be monumental. But even if the new Panama canal is not dug by nuclear explosives, the fact that it will run across the Isthmus at sea level rather than through a series of locks fills the project with unknowns. For no one can predict the effect of abruptly mixing the waters of two great oceans after they have been separated throughout four million years of geologic time.

What will happen when tidal surges in the Pacific, eighteen feet higher than the Atlantic, rush across the Isthmus bearing millions of tons of water with a different salinity, a different temperature, a different population of marine organisms? Thousands of species of sea animals may become extinct under the new marine environment. Climate may alter; the lives of nations may be blindly transformed.

The world ecosystems—the networks of organisms, from microbes to man, that live in precarious balance—are fragile indeed. Water, air, open space, living plants and living animals are all essential; we break their cycles, and sunder the web of life, at our peril. Do we act now to restore a livable environment to our planet, or do we allow the explosion of human numbers and the technological disruption of our global ecosystem to continue without forethought or control? Isaiah the prophet cried out when the desert sands, sterilized by generations of exploitation, were already advancing on Ur of the Chaldees and on the fertile fields outside Jerusalem:

> The earth also is defiled under the inhabitants thereof . . .
> Therefore the inhabitants of the earth are burned, and few men left. . . .
> And all her princes shall be nothing.
> And thorns shall come up in her palaces, nettles and brambles in the fortresses thereof; and it shall be an habitation of dragons, and a court for owls. [Isaiah 24:5, 6; 34:12, 13]

Two thousand six hundred years later, Albert Schweitzer, looking around at the Africa he loved and healed, echoed Isaiah:

> "Man has lost the capacity to foresee and to forestall. He will end by destroying the earth."

THE ATOMIC AGE ENVIRONMENT [2]

Environmental pollution is partly rapacity and partly a conflict of interest between the individual, multimillions

[2] From "Polluting the Environment," by Lord Ritchie-Calder, science writer and journalist, author of Living with the Atom and Common Sense About a Starving World. Center Magazine. 2:7-12. My. '69. Reprinted, by permission, from the May 1969 issue of The Center Magazine, a publication of The Center for the Study of Democratic Institutions in Santa Barbara, California.

of individuals, and the commonweal; but largely, in our generation, it is the exaggerated effects of specialization with no sense of ecology, i.e. the balance of nature. Claude Bernard, the French physiologist, admonished his colleagues over a century ago: "True science teaches us to doubt and in ignorance to refrain." Ecologists feel their way with a detector through a minefield of doubts. Specialists, cocksure of their own facts, push ahead, regardless of others.

Behind the sky-high fences of military secrecy, the physicists produced the atomic bomb—just a bigger explosion—without taking into account the biological effects of radiation. Prime Minister Attlee, who consented to the dropping of the bomb on Hiroshima, later said that no one, not Churchill, nor members of the British Cabinet, nor he himself, knew of the possible genetic effects of the blast. "If the scientists knew, they never told us." Twenty years before, Hermann Muller had shown the genetic effects of radiation and had been awarded the Nobel Prize, but he was a biologist and security treated this weapon as a physicist's bomb. In the peacetime bomb testing, when everyone was alerted to the biological risks, we were told that the fallout of radioactive materials could be localized in the testing grounds. The radioactive dust on the Lucky Dragon, which was fishing well beyond the proscribed area, disproved that. Nevertheless, when it was decided to explode the H-bomb the assurance about localization was blandly repeated. The H-bomb would punch a hole into the stratosphere and the radioactive gases would dissipate. One of those gases is radioactive krypton, which decays into radioactive strontium, a particulate. Somebody must have known that but nobody worried unduly because it would happen above the troposphere, which might be described as the roof of the weather system. What was definitely overlooked was the fact that the troposphere is not continuous. There is the equatorial troposphere and the polar troposphere and they overlap. The radioactive strontium came back through the transom and was spread all over the world by the climatic jet streams to be deposited as rain. The result is that there is radiostrontium (which did not exist in nature) in the bones of every young person who was growing up during the bomb-testing —every young person, everywhere in the world. It may be medically insignificant but it is the brandmark of the Atomic Age generation and a reminder of the mistakes of their elders.

When the mad professor of fiction blows up his laboratory and then himself, that's OK, but when scientists and decision makers act out of ignorance and pretend it is knowledge, they are using the biosphere, the living space, as an experimental laboratory. The whole world is put in hazard. And they do it even when they are told not to. During the International Geophysical Year, the Van Allen Belt was discovered. The Van Allen Belt is a region of magnetic phenomena. Immediately the bright boys decided to carry out an experiment and explode a hydrogen bomb in the Belt to see if they could produce an artificial aurora. The colorful draperies, the luminous skirts of the aurora, are caused by drawing cosmic particles magnetically through the rare gases of the upper atmosphere. It is called ionization and is like passing electrons through the vacuum tubes of our familiar neon lighting. It was called the Rainbow Bomb. Every responsible scientist in cosmology, radio astronomy, and physics of the atmosphere protested against this tampering with a system we did not understand. They exploded their bomb. They got their pyrotechnics. We still do not know the price we may have to pay for this artificial magnetic disturbance.

We could blame the freakish weather on the Rainbow Bomb but, in our ignorance, we could not sustain the indictment. Anyway, there are so many other things happening that could be responsible. We can look with misgiving on the tracks in the sky—the white tails of the jet aircraft and the exhausts of space rockets. These are introducing into the climatic system new factors, the effects of which are immensurable. The triggering of rain clouds depends upon the water vapor having a toehold, a nucleus, on which to form.

That is how artificial precipitation, so-called rainmaking, is produced. So the jets, crisscrossing the weather system, playing tic-tac-toe, can produce a man-made change of climate.

Industry and the Environment

On the longer term, we can see even more drastic effects from the many activities of *Homo insapiens,* Unthinking Man. In 1963, at the United Nations Science and Technology Conference, we took stock of the several effects of industrialization on the total environment.

The atmosphere is not only the air which humans, animals, and plants breathe; it is the envelope which protects living things from harmful radiation from the sun and outer space. It is also the medium of climate, the winds and the rain. These are inseparable from the hydrosphere, including the oceans, which cover seven tenths of the earth's surface with their currents and evaporation; and from the biosphere, with the vegetation and its transpiration and photosynthesis; and from the lithosphere, with its minerals, extracted for man's increasing needs. Millions of years ago the sun encouraged the growth of the primeval forests, which became our coal, and the life growth in the Paleozoic seas, which became our oil. Those fossil fuels, locked in the vaults through eons of time, are brought out by modern man and put back into the atmosphere from the chimney stacks and exhaust pipes of modern engineering.

This is an overplus on the natural carbon. About 6 billion tons of primeval carbon are mixed with the atmosphere every year. During the past century, in the process of industrialization, with its burning of fossil fuels, more than 400 billion tons of carbon have been artificially introduced into the atmosphere. The concentration in the air we breathe has been increased by approximately 10 per cent; if all the known reserves of coal and oil were burned the concentration would be ten times greater.

This is something more than a public health problem, more than a question of what goes into the lungs of the individual, more than a question of smog. The carbon cycle in nature is a self-adjusting mechanism. One school of scientific thought stresses that carbon monoxide can reduce solar radiation. Another school points out that an increase in carbon dioxide raises the temperature at the earth's surface. They are both right. Carbon dioxide, of course, is indispensable for plants and hence for the food cycle of creatures, including humans. It is the source of life. But a balance is maintained by excess carbon being absorbed by the seas. The excess is now taxing this absorption, and the effect on the heat balance of the earth can be significant because of what is known as "the greenhouse effect." A greenhouse lets in the sun's rays and retains the heat. Similarly, carbon dioxide, as a transparent diffusion, does likewise; it admits the radiant heat and keeps the convection heat close to the surface. It has been estimated that at the present rate of increase (those 6 billion tons a year) the mean annual temperature all over the world might increase by 5.8° F in the next forty to fifty years.

Experts may argue about the time factor or about the effects, but certain things are observable not only in the industrialized Northern Hemisphere but also in the Southern Hemisphere. The ice of the north polar seas is thinning and shrinking. The seas, with their blanket of carbon dioxide, are changing their temperatures with the result that marine life is increasing and transpiring more carbon dioxide. With this combination, fish are migrating, even changing their latitudes. On land, glaciers are melting and the snow line is retreating. In Scandinavia, land which was perennially under snow and ice is thawing. Arrowheads of a thousand years ago, when the black earth was last exposed and when Eric the Red's Greenland was probably still green, have been found there. In the North American sub-Arctic a similar process is observable. Black earth has been exposed and retains the summer heat longer so that each year the effect moves farther north. The melting of the sea ice will not affect the sea level because the volume of floating ice is the same as the water it displaces, but the melting of the land's ice caps and glaciers, in which water is locked up, will introduce additional water to the oceans and raise the sea level. Rivers originating in glaciers and permanent snowfields (in the Himalayas, for instance) will increase their flow, and if the ice dams break the effects could be catastrophic. In this process, the patterns of rainfall will change, with increased precipitation in areas now arid and aridity in places now fertile. I am advising all my friends not to take ninety-nine-year leases on properties at present sea level.

The pollution of sweet-water lakes and rivers has increased so during the past twenty-five years that a Freedom from Thirst campaign is becoming as necessary as a Freedom from Hunger campaign. Again it is a conflict of motives and a conspiracy of ignorance. We can look at the obvious—the unprocessed urban sewage and the influx of industrial effluents. No one could possibly have believed that the Great Lakes in their immensity could ever be overwhelmed, or that Niagara Falls could lose its pristine clearness and fume like brown smoke, or that Lake Erie could become a cesspool. It did its best to oxidize the wastes from the steel plants by giving up its free oxygen until at last it surrendered and the anaerobic microorganisms took over. Of course, one can say that the mortuary smells of Lake Erie are not due to the pickling acids but to the dead fish.

The conflict of interests mounts to a dilemma. To insure that people shall be fed we apply our ingenuity in the form of artificial fertilizers, herbicides, pesticides, and insecticides. The runoff from the lands gets into the streams and rivers and distant oceans. DDT from the rivers of the United States has been found in the fauna of the Antarctic, where no DDT has ever been allowed. The dilemma becomes agonizing in places like India, with its hungry millions. It is now believed that the new strains of Mexican grain and IRC (International Rice Center in the Philippines) rice, with their high yields, will provide enough food for them, belly-filling if not nutritionally balanced. These strains, however, need plenty

of water, constant irrigation, plenty of fertilizers to sustain
the yields, and tons of pesticides because standardized pedi-
gree plants are highly vulnerable to disease. This means that
the production will be concentrated in the river systems, like
the Gangeatic Plains, and the chemicals will drain into the
rivers.

The Role of Atomic Energy

The glib answer to this sort of thing is "atomic energy."
If there is enough energy and it is cheap enough, you can
afford to turn rivers into sewers and lakes into cesspools. You
can desalinate the seas. But, for the foreseeable future, that
energy will come from atomic fission, from the breaking
down of the nucleus. The alternative, promised but unde-
livered, is thermonuclear energy—putting the H-bomb into
dungarees by controlling the fusion of hydrogen. Fusion does
not produce waste products, fission does. And the more peace-
ful atomic reactors there are, the more radioactive waste there
will be to dispose of. The really dangerous material has to
be buried. The biggest disposal area in the world is at Hanford, Washington. It encloses a stretch of the Columbia
River and a tract of country covering 650 square miles.
There, a twentieth century Giza, it has cost much more to
bury live atoms than it cost to entomb all the mummies of
all the Pyramid Kings of Egypt.

At Hanford, the live atoms are kept in tanks constructed
of carbon steel, resting in a steel saucer to catch any leakage.
These are enclosed in a reenforced concrete structure and
the whole construction is buried in the ground with only the
vents showing. In the steel sepulchers, each with a million-
gallon capacity, the atoms are very much alive. Their radioactivity keeps the acids in the witches' brew boiling. In the
bottom of the tanks the temperature is well above the boiling
point of water. There has to be a cooling system, therefore,
and it must be continuously maintained. In addition, the
vapors generated in the tanks have to be condensed and
scrubbed, otherwise a radioactive miasma would escape from

the vents. Some of the elements in those high-level wastes will remain radioactive for at least 250,000 years. It is most unlikely that the tanks will endure as long as the Egyptian pyramids.

Radioactive wastes from atomic processing stations have to be transported to such burial grounds. By the year 2000, if the present practices continue, the number of six-ton tankers in transit at any given time would be well over three thousand and the amount of radioactive products in them would be 980 million curies—that is a mighty number of curies to be roaming around in a populated country.

There are other ways of disposing of radioactive waste and there are safeguards against the hazards, but those safeguards have to be enforced and constant vigilance maintained. There are already those who say that the safety precautions in the atomic industry are excessive.

Polluting the environment has been sufficiently dramatized by events in recent years to show the price we have to pay for our recklessness. It is not just the destruction of natural beauty or the sacrifice of recreational amenities, which are crimes in themselves, but interference with the whole ecology—with the balance of nature on which persistence of life on this planet depends. We are so fascinated by the gimmicks and gadgetry of science and technology and are in such a hurry to exploit them that we do not count the consequences.

We have plenty of scientific knowledge but knowledge is not wisdom: wisdom is knowledge tempered by judgment. At the moment, the scientists, technologists, and industrialists are the judge and jury in their own assize. Statesmen, politicians, and administrators are ill-equipped to make judgments about the true values of discoveries or developments. On the contrary, they tend to encourage the crash programs to get quick answers—like the Manhattan Project, which turned the laboratory discovery of uranium fission into a cataclysmic bomb in six years; the Computer/Automation Revolution; the Space Program; and now the Bioengineering Revolution, with its possibilities not only of spare-organ plumbing but of changing the nature of living things by gene manipulation. They blunder into a minefield of undetected ignorance, masquerading as science.

The present younger generation has an unhappy awareness of such matters. They were born into the Atomic Age, programmed into the Computer Age, rocketed into the Space Age, and are poised on the threshold of the Bioengineering Age. They take all these marvels for granted, but they are also aware that the advances have reduced the world to a neighborhood and that we are all involved one with another in the risks as well as the opportunities. They see the mistakes writ large. They see their elders mucking about with *their* world and *their* future. That accounts for their profound unease, whatever forms their complaints may take. They are the spokesmen for posterity and are justified in their protest. But they do not have the explicit answers, either.

Somehow science and technology must conform to some kind of social responsibility. Together, they form the social and economic dynamic of our times. They are the pacesetters for politics and it is in the political frame of reference that answers must be found. There can never be any question of restraining or repressing natural curiosity, which is true science, but there is ample justification for evaluating and judging developmental science. The common good requires nothing less.

OUR ENDANGERED COUNTRY [3]

The scientists and ecologists have been warning for years that earth's resources are not endless and that soaring population growth and blind disregard for the most vital resources of air and water could bring disaster. They have stepped up their warnings of pending disaster, because they

[3] From "Our Polluted Planet," by Gaylord A. Nelson, former Governor of and now Democratic Senator from Wisconsin. *Progressive.* 33:13-18. N. '69. Reprinted by permission.

believe that the end is virtually imminent. Every major watershed in America has been polluted by the unbridled expansion of business and industry and by municipalities unwilling to clean their wastes adequately before dumping. Lake Erie, an important fresh water supply for millions of people, is almost dead, and most other major bodies of water in the nation are close behind. . . .

Other events have been observed that have brought death to thousands of creatures living in and around the sea. Some were killed by the ugly oil spills off the coasts of California and southern England. Some, however, remain unexplained —with only the dead fish, birds, clams, or crabs, tumbling by the thousands in the surf, indicating that something serious was wrong.

There is almost no way to escape the poisons of pollution. Day after day the thin envelope of air that surrounds the earth is mixed with the belching smoke and soot of tens of thousands of industrial smokestacks and incinerators and the deadly fumes from millions of automobiles, buses, and trucks exhausting gases and lead particles from fuel into the air. Just how long the atmosphere will be able to absorb these pollutants cannot be predicted accurately.

The environmental threats have begun to jolt many Americans from their indifference and disregard for the severely limited natural resources of man. A recent Gallup Poll conducted for the National Wildlife Federation revealed that 51 per cent of all persons interviewed expressed "deep concern" about the effects of air pollution, water pollution, soil erosion, and the destruction of wildlife and natural resources. Most surprising was the fact that almost three out of every four of the persons interviewed said they would be willing to pay additional taxes to put a halt to these threats to life.

The Use of Pesticides

Even a limited survey of the ways in which man has been violating his environment demonstrates why the threat to life itself is so serious. The use of the deadly, long-lasting, poisonous pesticides is one of the most depressing examples. Each year, more than 600 million pounds of pesticides of all kinds are sprayed, dusted, fogged, or dumped in the United States—about three pounds for every man, woman, and child in the country.

The residues drift through the air, mingle with the waters to destroy aquatic life, and seep through the soil to contaminate the environment on a worldwide basis. Pesticide particles have been found, for example, in the tissues of reindeer in Alaska, in penguins in the Antarctic, and in the dust over the Indian Ocean. Several species of animal life, including the American bald eagle, the peregrine falcon, the osprey, and the Bermuda petrel are on the verge of extinction by pesticides.

A two-year national pesticide study completed recently by the United States Bureau of Sport Fisheries and Wildlife found DDT in 584 of 590 samples of fish taken from forty-four rivers and lakes across the United States. The study revealed DDT residues ranging up to forty-five parts per million in the whole fish, a count more than *nine times higher* than the current Food and Drug Administration guideline level for DDT in fish.

The threat of pesticides to public health and safety was made shockingly obvious . . . [in the spring of 1969] when the Food and Drug Administration seized 28,000 pounds of pesticide-contaminated coho salmon in Lake Michigan. The concentration of DDT in the salmon was up to nineteen parts per million; the accumulation of dieldrin, a persistent and more toxic pesticide, up to 0.3 parts per million. Both levels are considered hazardous by the FDA and the World Health Organization.

Dangerous levels of DDT and other deadly pesticides have been found in tobacco and fruit, and vegetable producers constantly must take care to avoid having their crops banned from commercial markets.

An irony of the whole pesticide saga is that, time and again, the bugs have come out on top. Hit the insects with a pesticide, and a few hardy generations later, adaptation has developed a new breed that is immune to it. Rather than seeking the obvious answer of an alternative pest control, our response has usually been to use greater doses of the same old ineffective stuff.

Yet, despite the urgent warning by responsible scientists of imminent environmental disaster and health hazards from pesticides, Federal agencies have failed dismally to face the threatening problem. Not one agency has taken any significant action that would lead to the goal of eliminating the use of persistent, toxic pesticides that was established six years ago by President Kennedy's Science Advisory Commission on Pesticides. ... [See "United Nations Efforts to Protect Our Environment" in Section V, below, for information about action against use of DDT.—Ed.]

Pollution from Nuclear Power Plants

In the deepening national crisis facing our rivers and lakes, a dramatic new pollution source is developing—the massive discharges of heated water from nuclear power plants.

On Lake Michigan alone, seven nuclear power plants, several with capabilities larger than any in the history of power generation, are scheduled to be in operation by the mid-1970s. Together with the output around the lake of existing plants fueled by coal and oil, the higher volume of expelled heated water will raise the temperature of all of Lake Michigan by several degrees in the next few decades.

In addition to the threatened change in the taste and smell of drinking water near some of the plants, the delicate chain of Lake Michigan aquatic life, already severely threatened by other pollutants, could be further upset. Algae growth is already a problem that could be greatly increased by the warmer water. Yet, incredibly, not one of the plants is installing cooling towers to reduce the environmental impact of the heated water on this vital segment of the Great Lakes chain—a major resource of international importance.

On a nationwide basis, 120 nuclear power plants will be installed within the next six years. By 1980, the electric power industry—with both nuclear and fossil-fuel plants—will be using one fifth of the total fresh water runoff in the United States for cooling. But the Atomic Energy Commission, which is charged with regulating the development of the nuclear power plants, said it has absolutely no responsibility to assure that the gigantic heat discharges will be controlled.

The tragedy of what is happening to the Great Lakes is clearly one of the ugliest examples of stupidity and greed. The pollution sequence has reached the point where Lake Erie is nearly destroyed, with Lake Michigan close behind, and Lakes Huron and Ontario gravely threatened. Only Lake Superior, the third largest body of fresh water on earth —almost three thousand cubic miles—is still clean.

Just how long Lake Superior will remain clean is highly questionable. The threat to its sparkling blue waters has begun. The Reserve Mining Company, owned by the Republic Steel and Armco Steel corporations, is dumping into these waters more than sixty thousand tons of wastes daily from its taconite—low grade iron ore—processing plant. It has been computed that, if the plant operates at current levels for the next forty years, it will dump into the lake 1 trillion, 881 billion, 600 million pounds of taconite tailings.

A Federal report concluded last spring that the waste discharge is already damaging the fragile ecology in the lake, is affecting the mineral content and the clarity of the water, and is destroying the already limited fish spawning grounds. There seems to be little question that the wastes are polluting the lake.

The Water Quality Act of 1965 and the Clean Water Restoration Act of 1966 were congressional declarations setting a national commitment to restore and protect the water quality of this country. Under the latter act, Congress authorized $3.4 billion in Federal aid for the period from 1968 to 1971 to begin the task. Congress recognized that the authorization was only for a minimal beginning and acknowledged that the job eventually would cost tens of billions of dollars.

Yet today, the water pollution control effort is in the same crisis condition as the waters of this nation. Efforts to implement the water quality standards face total collapse because the Federal aid commitment is not being met. In 1968, $450 million in Federal aid was authorized by Congress but only $203 million was appropriated. For 1969, $700 million was authorized, but less than one third that figure was appropriated.

The backlog of need continues to climb to gigantic proportions. Recent figures disclosed that $2.2 billion in Federal aid has been requested under pending applications for the construction of effective municipal waste treatment plants. These plants are needed to eliminate one of the most continuous sources of water pollution—soaring population growth makes the best systems inadequate in a short time. For 1970, the Administration originally proposed spending only $214 million of the $1 billion authorized, but under great pressure from Congress agreed to a substantial increase, and the ultimate appropriation may come much closer to the authorized sum.

Population Explosion and National Parks

... [In 1968] Congress recognized the hard fact that only a major infusion of new Federal funds would enable the creation of new national parks such as the Redwoods, and provide even a minimum of space and recreation for this nation's rampaging population growth. Congress amended the Land and Water Conservation Act to provide that revenues from outer continental shelf oil drillings—those beyond the three miles of shelf reserved to the states—would assure a minimum of $200 million a year for the next five years for the Land and Water Conservation fund.

But . . . [in 1969] the Nixon Administration . . . requested only $124 million for the fund, and it is unlikely that more money will be added either by Congress or by the Administration. The supplemental oil revenues, which . . . [totaled $76 million in 1969], are earmarked for the fund, but will be unappropriated and unspent, unless Congress and the Administration together take action. These oil funds could sit there indefinitely, as they cannot be spent for other purposes, while important available land is denuded of trees by chain saws and plowed into ugly, unplanned development by greedy real estate interests. Such delay destroys the encouraging starts made in conservation the last few years.

With demand for the nation's severely limited open space facilities already exceeding capacity, it is particularly disturbing to see Everglades National Park, one of the most valuable features of the National Park System, in grave danger of imminent destruction. In 1934, the 1.4-million-acre park was set up by Congress to be "protected in perpetuity" as a unique subtropical wilderness in rapidly developing south Florida. The concept, "protected in perpetuity," in the National Park statutes has always been comforting because it seems to rule: "Here is where we draw the line. Here we are endowing a priceless natural resource with a sanctity not unlike that of a church."

But, as is so often the case, the commitment of words and statutes is being swept away by the frenzied pursuit of profit. The Everglades Park is on the brink of destruction, final and complete. One conservationist predicts that, within ten years, there will be an announcement by the Federal Government that the Park is no longer worthy of the name and, therefore, wll be disbanded like an old military base, in the interest of economy.

It would be particularly appropriate for the Government to pronounce the doom of the Everglades because it has permitted Federal agencies—specifically the United States Army Corps of Engineers—working in direct opposition to the intent of Congress, to endanger the Park.

In 1962, the Corps of Engineers constructed a levee across the principal natural drainage way to the Everglades from the north and blocked the flow of water into the Park for two years. That water shortage brought the death of multitudes of fish, wildlife, and flora and began an unnatural succession of changes which may alter the unique ecology of the Everglades for all time. The only thing that saved the Park was a dramatic increase in rainfall in recent years, but that can be only a temporary respite.

Conservationists supported the Corps Flood Control Project, provided the Corps would insure that the flow of water would not be cut off from the Park. Without that protection, it is clear that the water—the life blood of the Park—will be choked off by the escalating industrial-municipal water demands of southern Florida or by drought.

In 1968, the Corps came before Congress for additional authorizations for the Flood Control Project and told the Department of the Interior, in writing, that the project would be regulated by rules designed specifically to protect the Everglades Park. But one year later, now that the Corps has its new authorization, it is refusing to implement that agreement and says it will wait for the "crunch" it sees—in thirty or forty years—before it acts. Such response is a blatant about-face, with obvious consideration for the wealthy land developers of south Florida who won't be happy until every square mile of the Everglades is dredged, filled, put under the blade of the bulldozer, and subdivided into suburban lots around dead lagoons stocked with fish from someplace else.

The Army Corps has already spent $170 million of the public's money for the project that is steadily and rapidly destroying the Everglades—and it is asking for $160 million more to further despoil the Park. If Congress and the Administration refuse to require the Corps to establish protective measures before any further Federal funds are spent, we might as well admit that the Government has no sincere concern for protecting the environment of this country, even when it has authority to control the situation. The call for private development apparently is too enticing. [See "The Assault on the Everglades" in Section IV, below.]

Polluting Our Ocean Waters

Perhaps man, with his rampaging breeding and indifference, has reached the point where much of the world he lives in will be nothing more than an area of poisonous waters and choking air surrounded by mountains of garbage and debris. With many municipalities already faced with a monumental problem of garbage disposal, it is estimated that every man, woman, and child in this country is now generating five pounds of refuse a day from household, commercial, and industrial uses. This refuse adds up to more than *365 billion pounds* a year.

Instead of using the country's impressive technology which made it possible to land man on the moon and develop supermechanical devices capable of solving astronomical problems, the typically American approach is to take the easy way—dump the debris and garbage in the ocean.

Why shouldn't the municipal governments and business and industry believe the ocean would be a good dumping place? The sea bottom is already being used for dumping radioactive wastes, and until the Army was stopped recently, some thoughtful military bureaucrat decided it would be a great place to dump discarded poison gases. Perhaps previous dumping has caused some of the mysterious events and massive sea kills I have described.

The oceans are not a limitless funnel that take the chemical wastes and other debris to a magical "somewhere else" where they can be forgotten. More than twenty years ago, Los Angeles found that its beaches were contaminated and had to be closed to bathers because the city was not sterilizing its sewage. It was also discovered that wastes pumped by England into the North Sea were damaging Grand Banks fisheries off Newfoundland. The Japanese, concerned about

their valuable fishing industry, have wisely banned dumping
sewage into the sea.

It is the economic profit to be found in the sea that at-
tracts and brings closer the threat of cataclysm which Dr.
Paul Ehrlich, a noted ecologist, projected recently. He predicted that unless current trends are reversed, the oceans
could end as a significant source of life in ten years with the
end of man coming a short time later.

The massive oil leak off Santa Barbara, California, which
killed fish and sea fowl could be the first dramatic warning
of this end. Other commercial ventures are under consideration as developers look to the possibilities of rich returns
from moving parts of crammed megalopolis to floating cities.
One developer is planning a floating jetport in the ocean
waters off New York City. Such a facility might well be beyond the reach of enforcement of any Federal agency regulations.

Unfortunately, there is a great deal of confusion and
litigation concerning whether various ocean waters are public, private, national, or international. It seems to be a wild
utopian dream that the world will be able to face the threat
to the oceans in any reasonable way in the face of the fact
that various government jurisdictions in this country cannot
get together to develop responsible control programs for a
simpler problem—domestic pollution. . . .

To date, eight thousand oil wells have been drilled on
the outer continental shelf. And little mention is made of
the fact that the outer shelf is really 823 thousand square
miles of undersea public domain, *owned by the people of
the United States*. This public domain was once much
greater. But in 1953, with the Submerged Lands Act, Congress gave outright, to the states, the first three miles of offshore seabed.

Today, greedy over the prospect of trillions and trillions
of dollars in potential shelf minerals, the East Coast states
are banding together to fight the Federal Government in

court for the undersea booty beyond the states' three-mile territory in a mad scramble for the public domain frontier.

Our undersea domain is not the only ocean area that is threatened. Landward, our coastline environment is becoming an unmanageable tangle of conflicting, polluting uses that eliminate wetlands, destroy shellfish and other valuable sea life in sensitive estuaries, wipe out beaches with unwise development, and degrade the natural values that make our coastline areas perhaps the most vital recreation resource in the nation.

The one heartening sign so far has been the courageous move by the state of New Jersey to freeze all action on purchase, lease, and use of state lands fronting on coastal tidal waters until completion by the state of a master plan for managing the coastal environment.

The same freeze should immediately be adopted for public coastal lands on the Atlantic and Pacific coasts, the Great Lakes, and the Gulf of Mexico. The Federal Government should halt all aid for development that would affect this environment until plans meeting national criteria are developed. And on the outer continental shelf—the vast undersea region extending beyond the coast—the Secretary of the Interior should grant no more leases of any kind until similar environmental criteria can be developed to protect this vital last frontier.

The President, with the advice and consent of the Senate, should appoint a group of independent specialists to develop the coastal land and water use criteria which the state plans would be required to meet. This group would also develop the outer continental shelf criteria. At least a three-year moratorium on continental shelf and public coastal land development will be required for orderly planning and adoption of the national criteria.

I will shortly propose legislation in Congress which will take these vital steps for protection of the coastline and ocean environments. Without such action, it will only be a brief time before the life-sustaining resources of our ocean are destroyed.

II. AN ATMOSPHERE FOR LIVING

EDITOR'S INTRODUCTION

The grave threat we face from air pollution is known now to all who live in our great cities with their recurring periods of smog. Pollution of the atmosphere also comes from radiation, pesticides which in turn affect foodstuffs and animal life, other pollutants, and the ever-increasing noise of our technological civilization.

The articles in this section deal with these issues both in terms of health hazards and the nuisance factor (as in excessive noise). The very real danger that pollution is affecting global weather patterns is touched on by a research chemical engineer, Eric Aynsley, in the second selection; and the possible dangers inherent in the production of nuclear energy are examined in the following article by a *Washington Post* staff writer.

Only passing reference is made to the problem of the insecticide DDT, discussed in the first and last articles in Section I. Once hailed as a boon in food and agricultural production, it will be virtually banned in this country by 1971.

Two articles from the *Bulletin of the Atomic Scientists* follow. They deal with the problem of the automobile in American life. It is, of course, our cars with their exhaust gases and fumes which are so overwhelmingly responsible for our most noticeable air pollution problems. Two further selections deal with noise pollution. The last item is a survey of the extent of air pollution in America given by a reporter for the New York *Times*.

AIR POLLUTION [1]

Carl Sandburg once saw Chicago as "hog butcher for the
world . . . player with railroads . . . under the smoke, dust
all over his mouth, laughing with white teeth." He meant
his poem to picture industrial America as manufacturing
a better way of life. But something—maybe it is the smoke
and dust—has made Chicago and most other cities stop laughing about the grime and start yearning for a breath of clean
air.

The Cost to Property

The cost of air pollution is staggering. When President
Johnson signed the Clean Air Act of 1965, he estimated the
economic costs of air pollution in America as $11 billion a
year. These costs are quite aside from costs due to medical
problems. They result from corrosion of industrial and
building materials; destruction of paint and other exterior
materials on homes and other buildings, both public and
industrial; need for cleaning (in a typical industrial city
twenty tons of dust fall on each square mile each month);
reduction of real estate values due to urban blight; increased
dirt and rust on cars; and fouling of recreational areas. All
this costs the individual citizen in this country about $60 per
year.

A typical suburban homeowner incurs losses of $200 to
$300 a year. These losses are due to costs for cleaning, more
frequent painting, and damage to shrubs, trees and grass.
What makes the situation discouraging is that the typical
suburb has no air pollution control program. Ordinances on
smoke nuisance are usually in existence, but they are rarely
enforced. Leaves are burned by individuals; building trash
is burned on construction sites; local industry discharges air-
borne wastes and solvents; incinerators pour out smoke and

[1] Article by Daniel Briehl, an aeronautical engineer at NASA's Lewis Research Center, Cleveland, Ohio. *America*. 120:580-2. My. 17, '69. Reprinted
with permission from *America*, May 17, 1969. All rights reserved. © 1969 by
America Press, Inc., 166 West 56 Street, New York, N.Y. 10019.

stench from homes and high-rises; and municipalities burn
trash in the open air in their city dumps.

Plants and vegetables suffer quite as much as property.
Sulfur and fluoride compounds in the air affect row crops,
flower gardens, parks, citrus groves, grains, cotton and fruit
trees throughout the country. It has been estimated that
$500 million is the price we pay for damage to crops alone.
(Paradoxically, if we continue to pollute the air, one serious
health hazard may be automatically eliminated, for air pollution also affects tobacco crops!) Areas near sources of industrial air pollution, even in the countryside, suffer from
poisoning of cattle due to pollutants.

Pollution ignores city and state boundaries. Selbyville,
Delaware, is a good example. The town consistently lost
population while the state's population continued to increase. The cause, once it was located, turned out to be as
plain as the nose on your face. It was a lard rendering plant
one and one half miles away, across the state line, in Bishop,
Maryland. Under the Clean Air Act, a Federal conference
was finally called to bring both states into action.

Paper mills are another offender, spreading hydrogen
sulfide and its smell of rotten eggs over neighboring towns
and villages. At nine hundred parts per million in air, hydrogen sulfide has toxic effects. Pollution from a paper mill
in Ticonderoga, New York, was bothering the people of
Shoreham, Vermont. With the two states' cooperation, the
Federal Government—again under the Clean Air Act—has
moved to curb it.

One of the least likely places one would expect to find
smog problems is amid the grandeur of the Rocky Mountains. Yet Denver, Colorado, is coming to the painful realization that a booming population, more cars and increased
industry mean more smoke. This city, like Los Angeles, owes
its misfortunes to the fact that its growth got ahead of its
weather and its topography....

Smog's meteorological accomplice is what is called a
temperature inversion. Normally, the air decreases in tem-

perature and density with the altitude. Smoke usually rides its warm air upward, dissipating in the atmosphere, and is blown away. Not so in a temperature inversion. In this weather phenomenon, a layer of warm air intrudes over lower cold air and acts as a lid, keeping the air beneath more or less stagnant. Meanwhile, minute by minute, the city below pours into the sky more pollutants, which all come down again about its shoulders.

Temperature inversions are brought about in two ways. Sometimes a warm front moves in over static cooler air. Sometimes, on a quiet, clear fall night, the ground radiates its heat skyward and cools the air at a low level, while warm air prevails above. Few areas in the country are immune to these two versions of the phenomenon.

In air-polluted cities, steel deteriorates two to four times faster than in rural areas. England estimates that one third of the cost of replacing its train rails is due to sulfur pollution. Dirty air deteriorates rubber, causing the side walls of tires to crack. It erodes the surfaces of stone statuary. Women walking in downtown Chicago have had their nylon stockings disintegrate. Air pollutants tarnish silver, affect leather and paper products, even eat into glass.

The Human Costs

But air pollution is more than a costly nuisance to property. It also has harmful effects on human beings. In the United States, an estimated 110,000 deaths each year are partly the result of air pollution. About 50,000 people die each year of cancer of the respiratory tract. An additional 60,000 die wholly or partly because of emphysema, chronic bronchitis and bronchial asthma. Though smoking is the best known cause of cancer of the respiratory tract, there is strong evidence that air pollution is at least as important a cause. This is because the same cancer-producing chemicals found in cigarettes are found in polluted city air. A person breathing the air of the average big city for twenty-four hours is supplied with as much carcinogen (cancer-causing chemical) as he is from one pack of cigarettes a day. In the largest cities, such as New York, pollutants in the air can provide the equivalent of smoking two packs a day. It is a matter of statistical record that the death rate from cancer of the respiratory tract in our big cities is twice that found in the country.

Today's fastest growing cause of death is emphysema. The result of this disease is a progressive breakdown of the air sacs in the lungs, caused by chronic infection or irritation of the bronchial tubes. Deaths from emphysema in the United States have gone up over 500 per cent in the past fifteen years. This increase is particularly marked in those states, such as California, that have a serious air pollution problem. The influence of air pollution on upper respiratory afflictions of all types was clearly shown in the experiences of Pittsburgh and St. Louis, where industry noted a sharp drop in medical absenteeism after air pollution controls were instituted. It is known that attacks of asthma routinely occur as a result of exposure to irritating dust and gases. Dirty air is often to blame, too, for headaches, irritated eyes, dizziness, coughing, nasal discharges, shortness of breath, sore throats and chest pains.

Controlling Air Pollution

The chief sources of air pollution are motor vehicles, factories and power plants, home heaters and waste disposal facilities. The number of motor vehicles in this country increases twice as fast as the number of people. By the year 2000, the use of electric power will increase five times. And unless drastic controls are imposed along with this increase, the amount of pollution will increase correspondingly. By that year there will also be a greatly enlarged population, 85 per cent of which will live in the cities. More people means more waste; higher standards of living mean that we will have to dispose of more waste per person.

Air pollution, however, can be controlled. The records of two American cities bear testimony to this fact. Los

Angeles—considered to have the best air pollution control program in the nation—has eliminated coal burning as a pollution problem and seeks to reduce pollution from oil burning. City officials want natural gas to be used as a fuel, though unfortunately there isn't enough natural gas to go around. The second city, Pittsburgh, had in 1940 a dust fall of 60 tons per square mile per month. By 1960, controls had cut it to 35 tons. By 1975, it is hoped, the fall will be down to 12 tons.

In terms of accomplishment in air pollution control, the state of California stands alone. This one state in a recent year spent more than half (57 per cent) of the $2 million budgeted by the various agencies for air pollution control in all the states combined. Most other states limit their pollution control activities to technical assistance and research. Only six attempt to enforce control programs. California employs over one third of the full-time personnel employed by all state control agencies in the United States.

There are eighty-five communities—with a total population representing less than one third of the nation—that have established some sort of city or county air pollution control agency. The total allocation of funds for these agencies is in the neighborhood of $8.1 million a year. Of this amount, 41 per cent is spent in Los Angeles County alone.

Smaller communities must look to their states for help in reducing local pollutants. But state programs are sparse and shoddy, and the small communities are likely to get no help at all. In fifteen states there is not a single law relating to air pollution control. In the remaining states, the laws are generally weak or unenforced, or they deal merely with smoke abatement or give the states no regulatory power.

Despite the Clean Air Act, however, there is considerable opposition to air pollution control. The greatest resistance comes from executives whose companies are among the worst offenders. For them, installing adequate control equipment represents a diversion of funds they would prefer to invest elsewhere. Even when an executive acknowledges that the problem of air pollution is real, he may oppose air pollution control on the grounds of cost. At the same time, some companies have reaped economic rewards by controlling pollutants. For example, oil refineries and power stations have a way to convert toxic hydrogen sulfide into salable sulfur and sulfuric acid.

Though a variety of techniques for controlling air pollution are available, putting them to use will take strong measures at the local level. First priority must be given to forming community action groups. Unless pollution control legislation is backed by active pressure groups, it is not likely to be passed.

Regional Programs Needed

Since air pollution freely crosses city and county boundaries, the larger the jurisdiction of a local program the more effective it usually is. Controls should be regionwide. Efforts should be made to establish and maintain consolidated districts among adjacent cities and counties. But cities cannot or will not work together in a satisfactory manner; and counties normally do not have charter powers to take over air pollution controls, and in any case are loath to do so since they already find it difficult to obtain funds for their other activities. Hence the most important source of any air pollution control is the state legislature. It is to the legislature that the public has to address itself.

The legislation to be enacted should provide adequate funds, and give adequate powers and authority over a meaningful area. "Adequate funds" means something like $12\frac{1}{2}$ to $16\frac{2}{3}$ cents per capita. The Federal Government will normally provide three-for-one matching funds for areawide authorities, so that the total funding will be 50 to 60 cents per capita. For an area of 1 million people, this will provide $50,000 per year, which is considered an adequate budget for air pollution control for such a population.

"Adequate powers" means that legal teeth should be put into provisions for air pollution control boards. Such boards should be able to enter premises without warning; they should be able to issue subpoenas, impose heavy fines, close down industrial or other operations, take people to court.

Pollution control regulations need to be strict. One enforcement power that should be written into pollution control laws is the power to grant or deny permits to operate equipment and processes. This is one of the most effective weapons in the arsenal of air pollution control agencies. Under such a system, a company may be closed down if it fails to demonstrate that it is at least making an effort to comply with pollution control standards. A prime advantage of the power to license is that it *prevents* pollution. Such an approach is much more effective than a mere effort to control existing pollution by court action. Injunctions, while useful for combating large and continuous violations, are too costly to rely on as a routine tool of air pollution enforcement.

A misdemeanor penalty is also a must in the rules for pollution control, with increasingly stiff fines for subsequent offenses. There is simply no other way to insure the compliance of private citizens who find it convenient to burn smoky fuels, trash and leaves.

Another important power of a control board should be the power over disposal of solid wastes. The board should be empowered to acquire landfill sites and/or build pollution-controlled incinerators by issuing revenue bonds; these bonds would be retired by payments from municipalities, charged pro rata as they used the disposal facilities.

A control board should have control of at least a countywide or a multicounty area. This arrangement is necessary to render the board eligible for matching funds from the Federal Government, and it is equally desirable from the point of view of air pollution control. Very large areas, however, may not be practical because of the amount of time board members would have to spend in travel.

Conservationists Versus Polluters

The boards set up to implement the law must be chosen from among the ranks of conservationists rather than of polluters. In Ohio, for example, the water pollution control board and the air pollution control board are both staffed in part by representatives of the polluters, namely, municipalities and industry; there are no conservationists on these boards. Desirable members of a board would be physicians, lawyers, engineers and others who have a demonstrated record of fighting for conservation. Such people should be chosen by public officials, such as judges, who are as far removed from party politics as possible.

Once a public group has decided that the state legislature should prepare legislation of this kind, its first act will be to draft such a law, with or without the help of interested legislators, and then conduct a campaign to have the legislation introduced and passed. This is an undertaking that all conservationists, church groups, civic groups and fraternal societies can join.

Local government should set a good example. In many localities, public facilities are among the worst offenders. A city government that has done nothing to correct smoking furnaces and noisome incinerators is not in a very good position to expect better of others.

One effective enforcement tool would be a tax on polluters for the use of the public air supply, much as a tax is levied for the use of a public sewer line. A tax of $100 for every ton of sulfur dioxide allowed to escape into the air would encourage a polluter to clean up promptly and would provide funds for the fight against air pollution. Auto registration fees might include a surcharge for vehicles lacking pollution control devices.

More states should exempt from property tax any equipment installed for pollution control. Tax abatement is offered by only six states, but this consideration would encourage compliance with control laws.

The Federal Government has made funds available for those who set up a local control program. The Clean Air Act of 1967 . . . [provides] two thirds of the cost of a program for a region consisting of one or more cities. For each increase in the budget of a local program, the Federal Government will subsidize two'thirds of the increment for cities, three fourths for regions. These subsidies in support of pollution control are revolutionary in concept and should be taken advantage of by regions throughout the nation.

The National Air Pollution Control Administration, which is under HEW [Department of Health, Education, and Welfare], now has a Community Support Program. The goal of this program is to support the Air Quality Act of 1967. This act provides for designation of air quality control regions. Responsibility for establishing and enforcing controls in the region rests within the state or states concerned. HEW provides the states with air quality criteria, containing detailed scientific information on the harmful effects of air pollutants on health and welfare, and with information on available control technology. This information then forms the basis for development by the states of air quality standards and enforcement plans, which become effective upon review and approval by HEW.

IS POLLUTION ALTERING THE WEATHER? [2]

For some years now, carbon dioxide has been under suspicion as a potential cause of major climatic alteration on a global scale. Carbon dioxide results from burning of all carbonaceous fuels, and since the turn of the century background levels of carbon dioxide have increased from 290 to 330 parts per million of air (ppm). The Earth's energy input is derived mainly from absorption of solar radiation, the Earth maintaining its temperature balance by reradiating long wave energy back to space. The absorption of in-

[2] From "How Air Pollution Alters Weather," by Eric Aynsley, a research chemical engineer at Illinois Institute of Technology Research Institute, Chicago. *New Scientist.* 44:66-7. O. 9, '69. Reprinted with permission of *New Scientist,* the weekly news-magazine of science and technology, 128 Long Acre, London, W.C. 2. © IPC Magazines Ltd.

coming radiation by carbon dioxide is small and changes in carbon dioxide concentration have no appreciable effect upon the transmission of energy from the Sun to the Earth. Nevertheless, carbon dioxide does absorb a major fraction of the long wavelength energy that is reradiated by the Earth. Consquently, increases in atmospheric carbon dioxide concentrations tend to reduce the heat loss from the Earth by diminishing the radiation loss from the Earth's surface. This causes increased ambient temperatures. Similar effects are observed in greenhouses, where the result of this diminished reradiation through glass manifests itself in the form of increased temperature.

Many scientists have tried to assess the increase of world temperature which could result from increases in atmospheric carbon dioxide levels. The problem is complicated due to the interaction of cloud coverage, atmospheric circulation and humidity with the Earth's radiation budget. Nevertheless, whilst making due allowance for the modifying effect of the Earth's cloud cover, it is estimated that with carbon dioxide levels at 600 ppm the Earth's temperature would rise by 1.5°C although again the interaction of global circulation and humidity could radically alter the conclusions. A change of 1.5°C in the Earth's temperature sounds insignificant until it is realized that the last ice age resulted from an average temperature drop of between 7° and 9°C.

Although the buildup of atmospheric carbon dioxide levels is not to be overlooked, recent observations have indicated a far more important aspect is the continual accumulation of atmospheric aerosols. This increase of atmospheric dustiness or turbidity has only recently been substantiated and if it continues unchecked can have devastating consequences. Measurements at the Moana Loa Observatory in Hawaii, which is remote from any local sources of air pollution, indicate a long-term increase in turbidity or atmospheric dustiness. Mr. R. A. McCormick and Mr. J. H. Ludwig at NAPCA [National Air Pollution Control Administration] in Cincinnati have shown increases in recent years of turbidity over Washington, D.C. of 57 per cent and over Switzerland the increase was 88 per cent and Dr. V. J. Schaefer and his coworkers at the State University of New York have documented many examples of large increases in atmospheric particulates of the order of tenfold during the last five years.

It is evident that Man's pollution of his own environment is increasing with world population, increased industrialization, urbanization and bad farming practices. Plumes of pollution emanating from the eastern United States can often be observed hundreds of miles out over the Atlantic. Similar air pollution zones are associated with Britain, Europe and the western coast of the United States. This atmospheric dustiness acts like an umbrella and shields the Earth from the Sun's radiation. Excessive dustiness can also initiate cloud formation, which both alters precipitation patterns and further reduces solar radiation.

The Consequences of Weather Changes

Little is known of the Earth's total radiation budget although this is the prime function responsible for both global wind and oceanic circulations. Evidence is beginning to accumulate that buildup of atmospheric dustiness is having a distinctly more profound effect than carbon dioxide accumulation. A slight reduction in the Earth's temperature has already been recorded in the last decade, and the Northern Atlantic ice coverage . . . [in 1968] was the most extensive for sixty years. On the global scale Dr. R. A. Bryson, a climatologist at the University of Wisconsin, suggests that pollution may even be responsible for the observed weakening of the trade winds and westerlies over the last decade. New comprehensive data on solar radiation is now becoming available from meterological satellite observations and this will enable a more precise determination of the magnitude and variation of solar fluxes.

Atmospheric dusts provide excellent centers or nuclei for cloud condensation, and very small particles are a necessary prerequisite for initial condensation of water vapor. Once condensation has been initiated the water drops grow from further condensation and coalescence. Depending on the prevailing meteorological conditions, either fogs or clouds are formed, the concentration of dust and atmospheric conditions dictating the extent and type of fog or cloud formation. An excess of dust produces small droplets under condensing conditions which grow from further condensation and coalescence and ultimately fall as precipitation. Information gained from intentional cloud-seeding experiments indicates that precipitation can be either increased, decreased, or not even affected. The final outcome of cloud seeding depends on the cloud type and prevailing meteorological conditions.

An example of increased precipitation from air pollution appears to exist at La Porte, Indiana, some thirty miles downwind from the smoky steel works of Gary and South Chicago. During the fourteen years up to 1965 La Porte had 31 per cent more rain, 38 per cent more thunderstorms and 245 per cent more days with hail than nearby communities. In fact, rainfall at La Porte increases in harmony with steel production rates at Gary!

Excessive dustiness in the atmosphere can also reduce rainfall under certain conditions when overseeding occurs. This happens when many small droplets, formed by condensation, do not fall to earth if there is insufficient moisture available to continue the droplet growth by condensation. Consequently what would have fallen as rainfall now stays in the form of clouds. A case in point of this reduction in rainfall has occurred in the sugar-producing area in Queensland, Australia. During the cane-harvesting season the common practice is to burn off the cane leaf before cutting and harvesting. This results in fires over extensive areas and large palls of smoke. The fine smoke particles have modified the cloud formation and hindered the rainfall process. A reduction of up to 25 per cent in the rainfall has occurred downwind of these areas, but there is no such effect in neighboring areas unaffected by the smoke plume. Similarly such effects have been reported by Dr. Schaefer to occur down-wind of Puerto Rico.

The ubiquitous automobile has a great potential to cause inadvertent weather modifications. The major offenders are components of the exhaust, which become highly reactive under intense sunlight, producing the well-known brown smog. The lead additives in petrol [gasoline] combine in the car exhaust and atmosphere with the small numbers of iodine molecules present and provide excellent particles for ice crystal formation. Dr. Schaefer has observed extensive ice crystal plumes in the winter around a number of large American cities.

Even steam and water vapor can alter the climate. The very large hyperbolic water-cooling towers that are becoming more popular throughout the United States, evaporate large quantities of water. These cooling-tower plumes can, if trapped under an inversion layer under stable weather conditions, generate and maintain a dense and persistent fog over wide areas. Already, flying at the Morgantown Airport in West Virginia has been disrupted by fogs which are believed to result from a cooling tower a few miles away. Ironically, it is planned to construct the world's largest cooling tower at a nearby power station! A further example of local climate modification by water vapor is Edmonton in Canada, which has more low-temperature fogs than neighboring areas. During cold winter spells the air cannot absorb all the moisture produced from the additional natural gas burnt for space heating. Thus extended periods of fog or ice crystal fogs are experienced.

The vapor trails associated with high-flying aircraft are well known. What is not generally known is that aircraft inject carbon dioxide, water vapor and considerable quantities of fine particles into the rarefied upper atmosphere. It is estimated that the high wispy cirrus clouds formed from jet contrails have already increased cloud coverage between North America and Europe by 5 to 10 per cent. These hazards of artificial clouds will be greatly increased as supersonic transport aircraft become a commercial reality. Dr. Bryson estimates that cirrus clouds could well attain 100 per cent coverage in these operational regions.

What If Cloud Coverage Increases?

Cloud coverage, especially at lower altitudes, is the most effective method of cutting off the Sun's rays and reducing the Earth's surface temperature. Global average cloud cover averages around 31 per cent. It is estimated that an increase of only 5 per cent in coverage of lower clouds would reduce surface temperatures sufficiently that a return to ice-age conditions could become a reality.

It is strongly suspected that particulate air pollutants are responsible for the many examples of inadvertent weather modifications I have discussed, though very few investigations of this problem have been conducted to date. Fortunately for mankind, the natural atmospheric cleaning processes are very efficient. Rain and snow are both effective scavengers of dust and certain gases, and only a few turnovers of the atmospheric water content are necessary to remove almost all air pollutants. But it seems that atmospheric particulates are associated with the major process of cloud initiation and related control of precipitation and reduction of sunlight, as well as the minor role involved in precipitation scavenging.

Man's knowledge of his ability to inadvertently modify his climate is still at best fragmentary. Insufficient is known about the long-term buildup of air pollutants, the effects and their interrelationships. A point of no return may be reached when air pollutant levels cause the climate to be modified to such a degree that a major irreversible global weather modification may follow. It is essential that mankind faces up to this problem to save his own atmospheric environment. Although detailed studies of air pollution and interrelated weather effects are necessary, the primary solution requires a continuing effort aimed at control and ultimate abatement of air pollution sources. Only then will a future of clear blue skies be assured.

POLLUTION AND NUCLEAR REACTORS [3]

"It isn't fair," complained an atomic industry public relations man at a University of Minnesota nuclear power conference, a conference inspired by the nuclear fight. "The militant conservationists are not doing much about the automobile. They're not all that excited over the old coal- and oil-burning power plants that are putting out sulfur dioxide and other ugly chemicals. But they're after us. They've made us a symbol."

"Indeed we have," a Minnesota militant replied. "If we can win this one, if we can arouse the people over this kind of pollution, maybe we can arouse them over others."

What one AEC [Atomic Energy Commission] commissioner terms the antinuclear movement began, in this state of lakes and streams, when Northern States Power Company —slogan, "Electricity Is Penny Cheap"—began building a big 560-megawatt atomic plant near Monticello, on the fresh-flowing Mississippi River just north of Minneapolis and St. Paul.

At first, all went swimmingly. Then Northern States Power sought a waste disposal permit from the new Minnesota Pollution Control Agency. The agency, needled by a set of young University of Minnesota biologists, engaged Dr. Ernest C. Tsivoglou, professor of sanitary engineering at Georgia Tech, as a consultant.

Tsivoglou, chief of radiological water pollution control in the United States Public Health Service from 1956 to 1966, acknowledged that nuclear plants in the United States commonly discharge only a small percentage of the radio-active contaminants that the AEC would permit. Northern

[3] From "Public Fights A-Power," by Victor Cohn, staff writer. Washington *Post.* p B 1+. O. 19, '69. Reprinted by permission.

States Power in fact said it would discharge no more than 1 to 4 per cent of the radioactivity that the AEC would allow.

Tsivoglou also acknowledged that the AEC has prudently set its standards in accordance with recommendations of both the Federal Radiation Council, representing several Federal agencies, and expert national and international bodies.

But he argued that knowledge of the effects of low-level radiation is highly imperfect, and future research may turn up new harm. He said that radiation should be more strictly limited in order to leave a reserve in case of future nuclear accidents or resumed atomic-weapon tests in the atmosphere. He looked to a day when atomic plants will dot the shores of the Mississippi and other U.S. waters, each adding its share of radioactive effluents. Northern States Power already is building two more big nuclear plants side by side at Prairie Island, south of Minneapolis-St. Paul, and has revealed plans for still more.

In effect, therefore, Tsivoglou recommended a set of standards at about 2 per cent of the AEC level. And in May [1969] the Minnesota Pollution Control Agency issued Northern States Power an operating permit specifying such standards.

The company said it could meet the new standards almost all the time, but occasionally might have to exceed them. It said it would have to modify its plant and shut it down more frequently to adjust to them, and additional annual operating expenses would be a prohibitive $3.5 million a year, making future electricity slightly more than penny cheap in the upper Midwest.

The Public's Role

Northern States Power has sued the state of Minnesota in both state and Federal courts, charging that its restrictions are unjustified and illegal. Nuclear power plant builders like Westinghouse and General Electric and even publicly managed utilities such as the Tennessee Valley Authority have rallied to Northern States Power's support.

And leaders of the congressional Joint Committee on Atomic Energy—in particular, Representative Chet Holifield (Democrat, California), chairman, and Representative Craig Hosmer (Republican, Illinois), ranking minority member—have sharply and impatiently questioned Minnesota's action.

Appearing on the University of Minnesota power conference platform, Hosmer firmly said that Congress has "preempted" the field of nuclear regulation for the Federal Government as one too complicated for state-by-state action. He and others said that where states have exercised radiation controls—as in uranium mining and in medical X-raying—they have done miserably.

But also, he charged, the Minnesota issue is "a big political football—certainly it is among the Minnesota delegation in Congress." He attacked "the professors around here who have been sounding off in the newspapers" and "Minnesota's underexperienced do-it-yourself stab at visceral regulation."

He said any complaints about radiation standards should go to the Federal Radiation Council. "They're not a subject for public rallies and placard making," he said, and "you can't have 200 million people deciding" them.

In reply, Dr. Barry Commoner of St. Louis—Washington University biologist and environmental crusader—said "informed public opinion" should indeed rule, even to accepting or rejecting a particular plant.

"The public is entitled to this vote," agreed Professor Harold Green of George Washington University's National Law Center, a former AEC associate general counsel. "Why, in a democracy, should the public not have the full opportunity to decide for itself, rationally or irrationally, what benefits it wants and what price it is willing to pay?"

Scientists Disagree

Conference discussion then centered on that price: the alleged hazards or virtual lack of hazards of power plant radiation. There were scientists on both sides.

Commoner and Dr. Arthur Tamplin of the University of California's Lawrence Radiation Laboratory at Livermore emphasized hazards. Commoner saw a possible U.S. increase in thyroid cancer of several hundred cases a year from power plant radiation escaping into the environment. Tamplin said nuclear plants now measure only overall radioactivity, but particular radionuclides—individual elements or their radiation-produced daughters—may cause greater than average harm.

He pointed to tritium, a heavy form of hydrogen, chemically inseparable from ordinary hydrogen. Once in human cells, it becomes part of the human heritage—incorporated into the DNA [deoxyribonucleic acid] that tells future cells and future children how to grow. He said AEC standards should be made more strict, individual radionuclides should be monitored and almost no plant wastes should be discharged into rivers. Instead, he said, all should be buried in atomic graveyards.

Dr. Stanley Auerbach of Oak Ridge National Laboratory and Dr. Merril Eisenbud, New York City environmental protection administrator and former AEC official, replied: "Man lives in a radioactive environment," absorbing radiation all the time from cosmic rays, building materials and the earth. Radiation from A-power plants can add only a few percentage points more. Despite many bugaboos, there is no laboratory or medical evidence of any ill effects of low-level radiation, they argued.

Other possible power-plant dangers were discussed: their considerable thermal pollution from the discharge of hot water, as well as possible plant accidents—"a remote danger," it was generally agreed, but a horrendous one. On each point, some speakers saw little problem, others peril.

When scientists disagree, concluded lawyer Green, the public and public bodies must decide. But the AEC, he maintained, has "a bifurcated interest," a "conflict of interest" in acting by congressional mandate as both A-power's developer and salesman and its government regulator.

He told how AEC officials, once they decide a plant is safe, become its enthusiastic supporters and defenders. "Clearly," said Commoner, "standard setting belongs in the hands of an agency concerned with all aspects of the environment," such as the Department of Health, Education, and Welfare's Consumer Protection and Environmental Health Services.

S. David Freeman, director of energy policy for Dr. Lee DuBridge, President Nixon's science adviser, agreed that this policy issue "deserves thoughtful consideration."

Again and again at the Minnesota conference, Representative Hosmer bristled. "It is time," he said, "that people quit painting the AEC as some kind of a nuclear Mafia engaged in a vast conspiracy." Even gentlemanly AEC Commissioner James T. Ramey said Minnesota "is making a mountain out of a molehill."

Some New Directions

Yet out of the Minnesota fight there may come some agreements or at least some new directions for nuclear power:

1. Commoner, Hosmer and Freeman agreed that environmental licensing and monitoring ought to encompass all kinds of power plants, not just A-plants.

2. Radiation standards in one way or another will probably be toughened. Northern States Power and the state of Minnesota are discussing a compromise which would in effect establish the right of a state to talk tough to power-makers. "There is not much question in my mind but that limits [of radiation tolerance] will be decreased as time goes

on," said Dr. Carroll Zable of the University of Houston, until recently chairman of the AEC's important Advisory Committee on Reactor Safeguards. "We are looking at them," Ramey conceded.

3. This high-energy civilization needs to keep looking at other sources of power, not just the atom. Unless more and more power is provided us, we will flick the switch one day soon but nothing will happen. "There is no doubt in my mind," said Professor Green, "that if in 1946 we had created a similar commission and joint committee to maximize the use of fossil fuels without polluting the environment, we would not need to rush so to build nuclear plants today."

4. The concern of the "new militant" environmentalists has only begun. "I assure you, gentlemen of the atomic power industry, you are not the targets," said Professor Commoner. "All polluters are."

ANTIPOLLUTION AND THE ELECTRIC CAR [4]

The electric power industry of this country has the beneficial characteristic of being what the economist terms an industry of decreasing costs, since it obtains large economies of scale in meeting increased loads. This has led to an almost continuous decline in the average rate paid by consumers of electricity, especially in constant dollar terms, and has, indeed, brought the industry to the point where it could inject the new element of electric heating into the space heating market.

I would not be surprised if, as a result of the policy directions already well developed in the efforts to improve the environment—superimposed on rising costs of debt capital—

[4] Excerpt entitled "Antipollution Technology: The Electric Car," taken from an address on energy and economics by Bruce C. Netschert, a member of National Economic Research Associates, Inc. *Bulletin of the Atomic Scientists.* 25:37. Ap. '69. Reprinted by permission of Science and Public Affairs (*Bulletin of the Atomic Scientists*). Copyright © 1969 by the Educational Foundation for Nuclear Science.

the power industry finds its long-term downward cost trend halted or even reversed. Would this be a bad thing? I don't know, nor does anyone else at this time. But let me use the electric automobile as an example of the implications I feel must be taken into account in the formulation of policy.

As you know, the electric automobile is looked on by many as a potential answer to the smog problem. I must confess I have a strong personal predilection for it. It makes sense to use a system that consumes energy only when it is in motion. It is quiet. It must, by its nature, be smaller than the palatial mobile palanquins we now drive, hence it would contribute mightily to easing the traffic problem. For the electric automobile to be commercial it is not sufficient that it have a battery that is economically feasible to manufacture and use: it must also recharge with electricity at a rate that is comparable with gasoline prices. Its fuel cost, in other words, must be competitive.

From the published information on the various proposals for electric automobiles it appears that, given the appropriate battery system, the electricity rates for charging would be competitive under present conditions. They might very well not be competitive, however, in 1990 or 2000, given the cumulative impact of environmental improvement measures on the power industry's costs in the coming decades. I don't know whether or not this is to be deplored. I certainly don't mean to imply that the electric automobile is the only or even the best solution to the smog problem. On the other hand, it would be deplorable if the fight for environmental improvement unintentionally and unknowingly foreclosed a potential development that could win one of the biggest battles.

What I suggest, therefore, is that those who are working to improve the environment should do their best to probe and appreciate the long-term implications of what they are doing, so that in their zeal they do not commit new mistakes in the name of remedying past ones.

In saying this I do not align myself with those who observe that there is no clear medical proof of the harmfulness of existing sulfur pollution levels in our urban centers; or with those who argue that there is no sense in equipping cars with devices to lessen exhaust emissions if the public is not going to maintain them; nor, especially, with those who protest that standards are being imposed too soon. I regard such objections as superficial.

I look, rather, at the more subtle aspects of the program to improve the environment, implications such as the long-term effect on electric rates I have just described—not so much the measures themselves as their direction. It is all too easy to set in motion economic forces which, once established, are difficult or impossible to change or remove. It is all too possible to build new rigidities into our economic system, which depends for its well-being on a flexibility that should be as great as possible in order to withstand unforeseen shocks and disturbances, both internal and external.

There are, as we all know, problems in environmental improvement that remain largely, if not wholly, unsolved. We can as yet do nothing about the nitrogen oxides. High-level radioactive wastes from power reactors are still handled on a temporary basis in stainless steel tanks which must be periodically replaced. There is the nagging matter of carbon dioxide and the greenhouse effect: we cannot yet tell if we are raising the average temperature of the entire earth, or, as has recently been suggested, whether we are permanently depleting the oxygen content of the atmosphere. I am confident the solution to each of these problems will, in its turn, come along. In the meantime we cannot stand still, though reasons can always be found for doing nothing. I am tempted to say that we must move with caution, but caution implies timidity and delay. Caution is also synonymous, however, with discretion and vigilance, and it is these qualities I urge in our actions in combating pollution.

AUTOMOBILES AND ANTIPOLLUTION MEASURES [5]

The thought-provoking "Antipollution Control: The Electric Car" by Bruce C. Netschert . . . [see preceding article in this section] calls attention to a very complex problem but examines only a narrow part of it: it does not touch upon other alternatives to the gasoline-burning automobile or upon the effects on air pollution of generating additional electricity for our cars. These are issues to be probed, if we are to exert "the discretion and vigilance" that Dr. Netschert urges in "our actions in combating air pollution.". . .

Information [on means to combat pollution from automobiles] is not easy to come by, although the automobile is the greatest single source of air pollution in the United States and consequently one of the chief concerns of the Air Quality Act of 1967. The Cleaner Air Committee of the Hyde Park-Kenwood community in Chicago, of which I am a member, has assembled a few facts and probably some misinformation on this subject. They are uncritically reported here in the hope that they might elicit clarification, comments and further information.

As far as the cities are concerned, the first obvious step to abate automobile pollution is to halt construction of highways and to develop good mass transportation. The advantages would be much greater than the disadvantages. If our inner cities were freed of traffic jams, fumes, noise, and unsightly parking lots, if our streets were made safe and pleasant for pedestrians, we might accept ungrudgingly the expanses of concrete that would spread near terminals to accommodate suburbanite cars or the costs of underground garages. . . .

A second obvious possibility is to allow only small cars within the cities. Not only do small cars burn less gasoline and for this reason alone produce less pollution (even though the percentage of pollutants in the exhaust is higher

[5] From "Cars and Air Pollution," by Laura Fermi, author of *Atoms in the Family. Bulletin of the Atomic Scientists.* 25:35-7. O. '69. Reprinted by permission of Science and Public Affairs (*Bulletin of the Atomic Scientists*). Copyright © 1969 by the Educational Foundation for Nuclear Science.

in small than in large automobiles), but small cars would also allow the traffic to move faster. Fast-moving cars produce less pollution than slow-moving ones: if an automobile's speed decreases from 40 to 20 miles per hour the pollution from that car approximately doubles. Furthermore, in bumper-to-bumper traffic a driver breathes the not-yet-dispersed carbon monoxide, hydrocarbons, nitrogen oxides, sulfur dioxide, lead and other toxics emitted by the car in front. In faster traffic a driver keeps at a greater distance from the tailpipe ahead. Is it possible to regulate by law the size of automobiles for city use? Some say that this would infringe upon a person's right of free choice, but we may counter by noting that everybody has a right to breathe clean air.

All 1968 models were equipped with devices to reduce emission of carbon monoxide and hydrocarbons in compliance with standards set under the Air Quality Act. But no standards were set and no controls required for nitrogen oxides. More efficient combustion, decreasing the amounts of carbon monoxide and hydrocarbons in exhausts, increases nitrogen oxides unless virtually all hydrocarbons (and carbon monoxide?) are eliminated. We would like to know whether all present control devices are based on more thorough combustion and result in increased production of nitrogen oxides. (Nitrogen oxides are especially dangerous under smog conditions because of photochemical reactions. What is known of their direct effects?) In 1970 stricter limitations for carbon monoxide and hydrocarbons are to go into effect, and control of nitrogen oxides is under study. But controls are so far compulsory only for new vehicles and it takes about ten years to renew the car population. The expectation is that by the mid-seventies the increased number of automobiles will offset the achieved and achievable emission reductions. New car designs will have to take over.

Substitute for Gasoline

One proposal calls for use of liquefied petroleum gas (LPG) instead of gasoline. We are told that LPG when burned produces smaller amounts of hydrocarbons and larger amounts of nitrogen oxides than gasoline but we don't know whether the reduction in hydrocarbons is greater than the increase in nitrogen oxides. We are also told that more LPG than gasoline would have to be burned (how much more?) because the proportion of air in the fuel mixture would have to be higher. LPG, now used to power some trucks and buses, is stored, moved and distributed under compression. It is claimed that in the hands of millions of persons unskilled in its handling LPG would constitute a considerable hazard: a recent explosion in a garage of the Chicago Transit Authority would seem to confirm the fear. Present LPG production is about 10 per cent of the gasoline consumption. If production could be increased (can it?) the automobile and fuel distribution system, including gas stations, would have to be redesigned.

Other automobiles of the future may get away altogether from the relatively inefficient internal combustion. The most promising designs are at present the gas turbine, steam engine, and electric car. All three have been built and tested. Their properties with respect to air pollution are known or foreseeable and encouraging, but all three are still beset by technical difficulties and high manufacturing costs.

As now conceived, both the gas turbine and the steam engine burn petroleum products, although other fuels, it is said, may be developed in the future. We would like to know what these fuels are and how soon they may be available. The gas turbine, an adaptation of the jet engine, burns petroleum gas, the steam engine burns kerosene. Emission of carbon monoxide and hydrocarbons from both will be much lower than from present cars not provided with control devices, and neither will burn lead. The turbine is said to have poor fuel economy; the steam engine averaged twenty miles per gallon of kerosene in a conventional mileage test. A report to Congress by the Secretary of Health, Education, and Welfare, who administers the Air Quality Act, states that both designs hold great promise for the period between the mid-seventies, when pollution from conventional cars will be again on the rise, to the mid-eighties, when the electric car may be ready to take over.

Creating More Electric Power

Among seriously considered automobiles of the future the electric car alone, to our knowledge, will not burn petroleum products. The electric car is Dr. Netschert's predilection. It was also the predilection of our committee and may be again if there is a change in the conditions under which electricity is produced. According to one estimate that we have not checked, electrification of our cars would double the present consumption of electricity. The demand would have to be met by new power plants. In our large cities of the East and Middle West we hear little about hydroelectric power, which now accounts for about one sixth of the total electricity in the United States. But we feel safe in assuming that hydroelectric plants will not play a major role in providing power for automobiles. Many hopes are pinned on fuel cells which generate electricity from the chemical combination of substances as clean and abundant as oxygen and hydrogen and might be used to power vehicles directly or to recharge their batteries. But fuel cells are said not to be "around the corner," and we don't know if and when they will be technologically feasible and economically attractive. So only thermal and atomic plants are left for realistic, short-term prediction.

Thermal plants are now among the worst stationary sources of pollution and it seems unlikely that completely clean operations will be achieved even if the industry were to spend more money on controlling its stacks. Besides, Dr. Netschert warns that the fight for environmental improvement may raise the cost of electricity and cause the doom of the electric car—a sad consideration in itself and even sadder for revealing the conviction that Americans will always put their purse ahead of their health.

The operation of atomic plants, on the other hand, is undoubtedly clean, and the experts say that sufficiently large plants will generate electricity at competitive rates. Most scientists assert that the huge plants they envision are perfectly safe, but a few recommend building them underground —a terribly expensive enterprise. Aside from considerations of danger from accidents or of economic factors, large atomic plants have inherent difficulties: their reactors generate enormous quantities of heat and create radioactive wastes on a very large scale.

Heat from reactors has already caused a rise in temperature in certain rivers. The Columbia River, for instance, "provided tremendous cooling capacity," according to a report of the Atomic Energy Commission, for operation of the Hanford reactors, and AEC studies show that rises of temperature in that river "persist for a hundred miles or more downstream." These temperature changes in our rivers may affect their ecology, and it is also conceivable that they may have secondary effects on land ecology. The life of the Great Lakes is already threatened by chemical pollution. To be exposed also to thermal pollution may be fatal to them. But if large atomic plants are built near Chicago, Detroit, Cleveland, Buffalo, and elsewhere, their reactors will almost certainly be cooled with water from the lakes or from rivers flowing into them.

It is well known that the water that cools reactors may carry along some radioactivity. The radioactivity in the Columbia River has always been within safe limits, but some phosphorus-hungry minnows ingested so much radioactive phosphorus that, at one time at least, its concentration in their bodies was 150,000 times as great as in the river waters. Perhaps it is possible to eliminate entirely the contamination of cooling water, but it is hard to see how heat pollution could be avoided or considerably reduced.

Progress in handling the by-products of atomic power has lagged way behind the advances in reactor technology. Still "under study" are fully safe containers for shipping spent fuel elements in large industrial operations, and radioactive wastes are still "managed" on a temporary basis. Dr. Netschert writes that high-level radioactive wastes are now stored "in stainless steel tanks which must be periodically replaced." Wastes are also placed in cement tanks that are stored underground or dumped in the ocean. The AEC is still seeking satisfactory and permanent ways of disposing of radioactive wastes. The 1968 AEC report is so optimistic about so many different and promising methods that it gives the impression that no foolproof method has yet been found. As long as the atomic industry is sufficiently small for scientists of excellence to keep an eye on it, we may feel that we are in good hands, but the prospect of very large quantities of radioactive wastes produced and handled by a rapidly sprawling industry is far from reassuring.

PHASING OUT DDT [6]

The warning sounded by Rachel Carson in *Silent Spring* is finally being heeded in Washington. After nearly a decade of evidence of the harmful effects of DDT and other hard pesticides on the country's environment and ecology, the Federal Government plans to outlaw these chemical killers except for essential uses in the next two years.

The agreement among the three concerned departments —Agriculture; Interior; and Health, Education, and Welfare —recognizes the peril to natural and human life caused by the insect killers. The HEW commission headed by Dr. Emil M. Mrak of the University of California reported evidence that cancer was produced in mice treated with heavy doses of DDT. Agricultural workers have become sick in the fields after breathing or touching certain pesticides. Toxologists have found that infants were ingesting twice the amount of DDT recommended as a maximum intake by the World Health Organization.

[6] From an editorial. New York *Times.* p 44. N. 14, '69. © 1969 by The New York Times Company. Reprinted by permission.

Since it was introduced into the environment about twenty-five years ago, DDT has performed wonders in the battle against malaria, typhus and other pestborne human diseases. It has helped to double the yield of cotton fields by controlling the boll weevil, saved fruit and other crops, and increased the production of livestock.

But . . . the price has been deathly high for various animal species and potentially high for unborn generations of Man carrying chemicals transmitted through mothers' milk. Thanks largely to the conservationists, the perils of the pesticides began some years ago to be discovered and exposed. Research of marine biologists showed that certain chemicals such as DDT pollute rivers and lakes and oceans, contaminating fish as a source of food; other scientists discovered DDT has a disastrous effect on the fertility of some bird species, such as the bald eagle.

The indiscriminate spraying of DDT has turned it into a worldwide contaminant. In the United States 100 million pounds are released into the environment every year, uncontrolled by laws except, recently, in a handful of states and communities where the miracle has at last been recognized as a menace. DDT and the other hard pesticides have a life of their own; toxicity can remain for years after initial spraying to contaminate the food supply.

It is essential that administrative action be taken at local and state as well as the Federal level. But meanwhile, Secretary Finch's announcement is a giant step forward in reducing the menace to all living creatures of the long-lasting poisons that have been used with such careless and ignorant abandon for so many years.

NOISE POLLUTION: A HEALTH HAZARD [7]

Man, in creating technics and devices to help build his cities, speed his travels, better his life, has unwittingly pro-

[7] From "A Jet-Age Health Hazard," by William H. Stewart, M.D., former Surgeon General, United States Public Health Service. *Trial.* 5:53-4. F.-Mr. '69. Reprinted by permission.

duced a number of inherent dangers as by-products of his inventiveness.

One of these is excessive noise. The sounds of progress can, unfortunately, be deafening.

Noise, which can be defined as any unwanted sound, has been a constant accompaniment of progress since the start of the industrial revolution. It has reached a crescendo in the sound of today's airplanes and trucks, jackhammers and earthmovers, air conditioners and vacuum cleaners, booming hi-fi's and blaring sirens. In this century we are seeing a fantastic growth in technology at a time when America has become primarily an urban rather than an agrarian nation. Thus, the devices which pollute our environment with noise are on the increase at a time when our population has become concentrated in areas where the noise levels are highest.

Attempts to control noise have failed to diminish the increasing din the average American is asked to endure. Many cities have imposed noise limits on industry while allowing unrestricted clamor from construction machinery and motor vehicles. Other municipalities, endowed with noise-conscious lawmakers who attempt to quiet the community, have found themselves unable to control noise from nonlocal sources with local ordinances. Aircraft and highway noises are good examples.

Efforts to control noise are not new. Records show that in the early 1800s, in Great Britain, stagecoach drivers were arrested because the sounds from their carriages drowned out church services. In the early 1900s, in this country, city planners took noise into account when setting up zoning ordinances. The United States Supreme Court, in 1926, took note of zoning as a means to "decrease noise and other conditions which produce nervous disorders." Four years earlier, in Newark, New Jersey, school officials requested "noiseless" pavements in the vicinity of schools.

In general, however, noise control has fallen short, largely because the problem has been underestimated or ignored. There is a widespread belief that noise is an inevitable aspect of modern civilization—a necessary nuisance.

But the facts show that from a medical standpoint noise is not merely a nuisance that we can learn to live with. Inevitable as it may seem in a highly technical, industrial society, noise is a health hazard which must ultimately be controlled. And today noise is reaching such levels that we cannot afford to wait much longer. . .

What Health Hazards?

Excessive noise causes *hearing loss*—actual physical damage to the cells of the ear. Hearing ability of selected groups of industrial workers who are exposed to high noise levels is significantly poorer than that of comparable nonexposed groups. We have reason to believe that perhaps half the machines in industrial use produce noise levels intense enough to pose a hazard to the hearing of exposed workers. Yet, in the vast majority of states, laws to compensate workers for noise-induced hearing loss are woefully inadequate at the present time.

Noise can cause *physiological changes*—cardiovascular, glandular, and respiratory effects reflective of a generalized stress condition. This effect is well explained by Dr. John Anthony Parr (. . . *Congressional Record*—House, April 21, 1966):

Why should noise upset our health? Well, it's all due to an inborn alarm system we have. A sudden loud noise spells danger and we react. In fact we automatically get ready to defend ourselves or flee. Our muscles tense and we jerk, our abdominal blood vessels contract to drive extra blood to our muscles and this produces that feeling of the stomach turning over, and in an instant the liver releases stores of glucose to provide fuel for the muscles which may have to fight or run. This internal upheaval if repeated again and again is exhausting physically and mentally, and ultimately can cause a nervous breakdown, and then it is but a step to contracting one of the stress diseases.

Noise can cause other *less well defined health detriments* —disturbing concentration at work, or relaxation at leisure.

Also, noises which obscure warning signals, or impair communication, can certainly become hazards.

Admittedly, there are vast areas where we do not know the organic and psychological effects of noise. In fact, we have hardly begun to explore all the ramifications of our noise problem. There are many potentially fruitful avenues for research which merit immediate attention and high priority—physiological studies, psychological studies, investigations of the epidemiology of noise damage in the community, and many more.

Meanwhile, as in the examples I have mentioned, we have ample data to show that noise is a health hazard. It is not presumptuous to assume we will discover more "noise hazards" as our knowledge on the subject increases. . . .

We in the United States Public Health Service are charged with protecting the health of the citizens of this nation. Health—as defined by the World Health Organization—is not simply the absence of diseases, but a matter of physical, mental and social well-being. Our concern for human health is a concern for the quality of human living. We would not be living up to our responsibilities to the people of America if we sought a narrower definition.

Because of this, the Public Health Service was instrumental in setting up the First National Conference on Noise as a Public Health Hazard in Washington . . . [in June 1968]. Noted experts representing government agencies, scientific and medical institutions, industry, and private groups met for two days on all aspects of the noise problem.

The Conference was an unqualified success, even though it produced no immediate, absolute answers. But the Noise Conference did provide an excellent starting point, a look at the present state of human knowledge on the subject and an indication of what steps must be taken. It produced, for the first time in one package, a view of all the varying facets of the problem of noise in a modern society. From this package will come clear directions as to what research activities are needed, as well as what guidelines should be used by government, industry, and commerce to help control and regulate noise.

The issue is the harnessing of technology to human ends. Good effects of each new product of technology must be carefully weighed against the bad effects. Noise is unquestionably one of the bad effects. Our society's highest aspiration is individual self-fulfillment. When the individual is jolted, distracted, or disturbed—in work or leisure—by noise that need not assail him, his very fundamental right to the pursuit of that fulfillment is impaired. Therefore, for every new possibility that technology offers, the question must be put: for the benefit of whom, and at what collateral hazard to the beneficiary and to others?

The Noise Conference was a very encouraging step in the right direction. Other such steps are being taken. New legislation, on national, state, and local levels, appears in the offing. Public awareness is mounting. Letters are being written to editors and to congressmen. Citizen groups—many comprising distinguished scientists, writers, and conservationists—are being formed.

These movements must become stronger in our jet-age world than the noise they seek to abate. Noise is not something we are going to be able to live with. It must be controlled, on the drawing boards and in the courts.

PERVASIVE NOISE POLLUTION [8]

The sources of noise today seem almost limitless. From the kitchen in the modern home comes a cacophony that would require ear defenders in industry to prevent hearing loss. In a series of measurements made in one kitchen, a

[8] From "Environmental Noise Pollution: A New Threat to Sanity," by Donald F. Anthrop, a research chemist at Lawrence Radiation Laboratory, Berkeley, California. *Bulletin of the Atomic Scientists.* 25:11-16. My. '69. Reprinted by permission of Science and Public Affairs (*Bulletin of the Atomic Scientists*). Copyright © 1969 by the Educational Foundation for Nuclear Science. (In November 1969 the FAA issued regulations detailing noise abatement requirements for new aircraft. Regulations for existing aircraft were to be issued in 1970.—Ed.)

dishwasher raised the noise level in the center of the kitchen from 56 to 85 decibels, while the garbage disposal raised it to more than 90 decibels. A food blender produces about 93 decibels. Power lawn mowers and leaf rakers, outside air conditioners, and power tools such as saws contribute to the noise in the home. But for most Americans, construction and transportation sources, particularly trucks, motorcycles, sports cars, private airplanes and helicopters as well as commercial jets and military aircraft, are the most serious offenders.

Construction and Transportation Noise

Particularly in large cities, construction noise is a very substantial and seemingly continuous nuisance. This noise can be substantially reduced with existing technology and without great cost. In December 1967, Citizens for a Quieter City in New York demonstrated a muffled air compressor developed in Great Britain and used there for the past five years which reduced the noise level from 86 to 79 decibels at a distance of twenty-five feet. The compressor is enclosed in a plastic housing lined with foam plastic. This organization also demonstrated a muffled jackhammer which produced significantly fewer decibles. . . .

Transportation constitutes the principal source of noise in most American cities. There are now 81 million privately owned passenger cars in the United States compared with 25.5 million at the end of World War II. Each year 7 million of these wear out or are junked, but in the past few years an average of 10 million new ones have been produced or imported each year. Thus, the number of automobiles is increasing at the rate of nearly 4 per cent a year. As if 81 million automobiles didn't create enough congestion and noise, there are also 2.4 million motorcycles and 16.5 million trucks.

Motor vehicle noise has been primarily an urban problem. In a recent study of noise in Boston schools, a mean reading of 78 decibels was recorded in a school playground in downtown Boston. In Wellesley, a suburb of Boston, the noise level in the school playground was only 58. Thus, children in the city school were exposed to a noise intensity 100 times greater than the suburban Wellesley children. But the rapid increase in the number of motor vehicles, the production of larger and noiser trucks, the construction of the interstate highway system, and the exodus of people from city to suburb has increasingly brought noise pollution to suburban areas and the countryside.

One of the most comprehensive noise surveys ever made was the London survey in 1961. Noise measurements were made at 540 locations in central London, and 1,400 residents at those locations were interviewed. At 84 per cent of the points traffic noise predominated. About one third of the people specifically mentioned motor vehicle noise as a major irritant. Furthermore, traffic noise appeared to be as important an annoyance as all other noises together.

A number of surveys have established beyond doubt that the noise problem near high-speed highways arises principally from trucks, motorcycles, and sports cars. In 1964 the California Highway Patrol conducted a series of tests along California highways in which noise levels of 25,351 passenger cars, 4,656 gasoline trucks, and 5,838 diesel trucks were measured. Noise levels of the passenger cars, measured 50 feet from the road, varied between 65 and 86 decibels with the average falling at about 76. On the other hand, noise levels for diesel trucks ranged from 68 to 99 decibels with the average at about 87.

Antinoise Laws

The results of these various surveys demonstrate quite clearly that in order to achieve quieter living conditions, cities must reduce motor vehicle noise. Yet governments at all levels have thus far failed to achieve any meaningful reductions. In 1965 the State of New York enacted a law limiting the noise a motor vehicle can produce at a distance of 50 feet to 88 decibels while traveling 35 miles per hour. In 1967 California enacted legislation which sets a limit of 92 decibels for motorcycles and trucks of three tons gross or more, traveling at speeds above 35 miles per hour. All other motor vehicles are limited to 86 decibels. That these limits are much too high is suggested by the fact that in 1961 California hired an acoustical consulting firm to make a survey of motor vehicle noise and to recommend limits consistent with existing technology and currently available noise measuring techniques. The firm recommended maximum limits of 87 decibels for trucks and motorcycles and 77 for other motor vehicles.

Even these lower limits were deemed to be easily attainable with existing technology. Furthermore, no valid argument has been advanced to justify higher noise limits for motorcycles than for passenger cars. There is no reason why a 50-horsepower motorcycle should be allowed to make as much noise as four 300-horsepower Cadillacs. Yet the new California noise law permits precisely this situation. Worse yet, the law is not being enforced, particularly with respect to motorcycles, which have become a real threat to sanity in city and back country alike....

The future of our cities depends in no small measure on how successful we are in reducing traffic noise and congestion. Three approaches are open to us: (1) reduce the noise of the source; (2) eliminate the source through the use of quiet, underground mass transit systems; (3) reduce the noise near freeways by depressing the roadway or constructing a sound barrier along the right-of-way....

Aircraft Noise

Since there are now nearly 1,200 jet airliners, about an equal number of piston aircraft, and more than 100,000 private airplanes in service in the United States, the aircraft noise problem has become very widespread. Today millions of Americans are affected by this aural assault: Congressmen Benjamin Rosenthal and Herbert Tenzer whose Long Island communities lie under the flight paths for La Guardia and

Kennedy have warned that the mood of their constituents has become one of desperation, not just unhappiness.

The courts have held that insofar as the operation of aircraft is concerned, the Federal Government has preempted the field. A 1963 ordinance of Hempstead, Long Island, which regulated the altitude and flight path of aircraft while over the city was ruled invalid in a 1967 court suit. Ordinances such as the recent one passed by the city of Santa Barbara banning supersonic flights over the city also would probably be declared invalid in a court test.

Noise levels in some communities near our major airports have become so intolerable that many residents cannot continue to live in those communities. Lawsuits totaling $200 million are pending in the courts. . . . One does not have to be directly under the flight path of a large jet on takeoff in order to receive an ear-splitting roar. When a 707-320B jet is four miles from the point of brake release at the end of the runway it has attained an altitude of about 800 feet and the noise level on the ground one half mile on either side of the flight path is approximately 85 decibels.

Federal officials should not be surprised by the magnitude of the present problem. In 1952 President Truman received a report, "The Airport and Its Neighbors," from his Airport Commission. The Commission said greater consideration should have been given residents living in an area when airports were first built and that civil and military officials should make much greater efforts to reduce takeoff noise over residential areas.

But Federal officials are just now beginning to do something about the problem. In August 1968, President Johnson signed into law a measure requiring the Federal Aviation Administration to undertake control and abatement of aircraft noise. The FAA was not particularly eager to have this responsibility, for the law appears to make the FAA liable for damage suits arising from aircraft noise.

The FAA has initiated noise control procedures at some airports, but until quieter engines are built, there is not a great deal it can do with regard to jet transport noise. The noise control procedures that have been implemented are directed almost solely at reducing the noise level in communities lying directly under the flight path while the plane is at low altitude. While reductions have been achieved in such communities, the result has often been to spread the noise around to other communities.

This is precisely what has occurred at the Washington, D.C., National Airport where the FAA requires departing aircraft to climb as quickly as possible to 1,500 feet and then cut back the power and follow the Potomac River northward. Flights over the White House, the Capitol, the Washington Monument, and the U.S. Naval Observatory are prohibited. But since Washington National Airport is just across the Potomac River from the Lincoln Memorial, central Washington is still bombarded by the constant roar of jets, and communities such as Georgetown are now directly under the flight path. Why should residents of Georgetown be subjected to the noise while congressmen on Capitol Hill are protected from the din? If the congressional office buildings rather than residential communities were under the flight path, Congress would long ago have taken steps to end the nuisance.

The solution to the aircraft noise problem in the District of Columbia is to close Washington National Airport. Few people presently use Dulles [International Airport] because it is so far from the city, but it would be much more attractive if a rapid transit system connected the airport with downtown Washington. Furthermore, a substantial percentage of the traffic at Washington National Airport consists of Washington-New York and Washington-Boston commuter service. If high-speed rail service were available between these points, this traffic could be almost eliminated.

Getting at the Source

While flight procedures can bring relief to some communities, the only solution to the aircraft noise problem lies in quieting or eliminating the source. NASA [National Aeronautics and Space Administration] is financing research and development to develop a new "quiet engine." Preliminary tests indicate the new quiet engine will reduce takeoff noise by 15 decibels. In static tests with a Pratt and Whitney J-57 engine, Boeing claims to have obtained a noise reduction of nearly 40 decibels by use of acoustical linings in the engine. There are reports that the proposed European airbus will use advanced engines which will produce a 75 decibel noise level on takeoff. For comparison, the Boeing 707-320B in normal operation (that is, in the absence of FAA noise control procedures) produces about 107 decibels on takeoff. Clearly, then, the manufacturers can build quieter aircraft if they are forced to do so.

When can we expect some relief? Manufacturers say the giant Boeing 747, scheduled for late 1969, is already in production and cannot be fitted with new engines even if they were available. The 747 is expected to produce a 100 decibel noise level on takeoff. The airlines argue that to retrofit existing turbojets with the new quiet engine would cost $6 million per plane and that they cannot afford it. Thus, if the present trend continues, we cannot expect any relief before the late 1970s. But by that time any noise reduction will be partly offset by the doubling of air traffic expected between now and 1975. The fact is that the present exasperating noise problem exists because the aircraft manufacturers and the airlines have operated on the basis of their own short-range economic interests and have failed to devote the efforts and resources needed to solve it.

If the already grave situation is not to become worse, some bold steps will have to be taken:

1. The Federal Government should provide a greatly increased funding level for quiet engine research so that takeoff noise will be reduced by 40, not 20 decibels.

2. Whenever a substantially quieter engine is developed, the FAA should require existing aircraft to be retrofitted with the new engine. If the airlines cannot afford the cost

without increasing fares, then fares should be increased. The small percentage of the population that uses the airlines should be required to assume part of the burden for providing a livable environment for the millions of people who suffer from the noise but derive no economic benefit from it.

3. Particularly in densely populated areas such as the Northeast Corridor, the Chicago-Pittsburgh region, and the San Diego-San Francisco corridor, high-speed rail transportation could substantially reduce air traffic.

4. Future airports should be planned according to the principles used at Dulles International Airport and the new one now being planned for Dallas where 18,000 acres are being purchased to prevent encroachment of residential dwellings.

5. New airports should be located twenty or thirty miles from the metropolitan area, as Dulles International Airport is, and serviced by high-speed surface transportation. . . .

While a feeble first step has been taken to reduce the noise produced by civilian aircraft, the deafening roar of military planes continues unabated, for the FAA does not have jurisdiction over military planes or flight operations. The Department of Defense has made no effort to develop quieter jet aircraft, claiming that it cannot afford the weight penalty that quieter engines would impose. Instead of making a serious effort to reduce noise levels in communities near military installations, Defense has embarked upon a public relations campaign to convince the American public that they should not only tolerate but welcome this assault on their eardrums because the military establishment is defending them. This country's military brass seems quite willing to destroy our environment in the name of defending it.

A case in point is the Alameda Naval Air Station which lies adjacent to the city of Oakland, California, in the very heart of a metropolitan area. Over 1.75 million people live within twelve miles of the runway. Berkeley and Oakland residents frequently find themselves rudely awakened early Sunday morning by jets streaking over the East Bay hills with afterburners blazing. If an aroused public demands the closure of some of these poorly situated installations, perhaps the Defense Department will be motivated to develop quieter aircraft.

Sonic Boom and the SST

The worst is yet to come when—and if—Boeing's supersonic transport (SST), built with Federal financing, goes into service in the 1970s. Whenever a plane flies faster than the speed of sound (about 344 meters per second) it generates shock waves which trail out behind the plane on both sides of its path. When these shock waves intercept the earth, they produce the thunderclap we call sonic boom. Typically the boom is felt along a belt that extends forty miles on each side of the plane's flight path. The severity of the boom depends on the plane's size and altitude, but there is no known way to eliminate the boom itself. There exists a common misconception that this sonic boom is produced only once when the plane first exceeds the speed of sound. In fact, it is produced continuously along the plane's path while it is in supersonic flight.

The whole SST program places in serious question the commitment of the FAA, the Department of Transportation and Congress to noise reduction. Thus far, Congress has appropriated $653 million for SST. Worse yet, on July 11, 1968, the Senate defeated an amendment to the Aircraft Noise Abatement Act which would have prohibited the SST from flying at supersonic speeds across continental America. The proponents of SST in Congress argued that prohibition of overland flights was unnecessary because the FAA probably would not permit such flights anyway. But the very fact that Congress was unwilling to legislate against sonic boom indicates overland flights by the SST are anticipated. And since the FAA is the agency responsible for the direction and funding of the entire SST development program, asking it to regulate sonic boom is like putting the fox in the chicken coop. The attitude of the Department of Transportation on the sonic boom issue is illustrated in a statement made by Major General Jewell C. Maxwell, the chief of the SST program: "We believe that people in time will come to accept the sonic boom as they have the rather unpleasant side effects which have accompanied other advances in transportation."

This is a myth which so far has survived scientific evidence to the contrary. Aircraft noise studies have shown that people become more intolerant of jet aircraft as the number of flyovers or the duration of each flyover is increased.

In order to assess public acceptance of sonic boom, the FAA conducted tests in Oklahoma City in 1964. During a six-month period, 1,253 supersonic flights were made over the city. Oklahoma City was one of the most favorable locations the FAA could have chosen to get public acceptance of sonic boom since nearly one third of the city's residents depend on the aviation industry for their living. Furthermore, no sonic booms were made at night—the really critical test. Yet 27 per cent of the people said they could never learn to live with the sonic boom and over 4,900 residents filed damage claims against the FAA. Most people found the booms more irritating at the end of the tests than at the beginning.

Operation of the SST over continental United States would not only shatter the solitude of nearly every park and wilderness area in the country, but could do extensive damage to some of these places as well. Between August 11 and December 22, 1966, some eighty-three sonic booms, several of which caused extensive damage, were recorded in Canyon de Chelly National Monument, Arizona. One of these booms loosened an estimated eighty tons of rock which fell on ancient Indian cliff dwellings and caused irreparable damage. Damage has also been reported in Bryce Canyon National Park, Utah.

Canada has already banned the operation of supersonic aircraft over its provinces. Both Switzerland and West Germany have indicated they will prohibit supersonic flights within their borders if their citizens complain.

Boondoggle Program

The whole SST program is an economic boondoggle, the prime beneficiary of which is the aircraft manufacturing industry. The FAA has committed $1.3 billion or about 83 per cent of the estimated development cost and Congress has already appropriated half this amount. But low cost estimates and delays in the program now indicate the cost to the Federal Government will be at least $3.5 billion before the first plane is sold. The FAA talks glowingly of estimated sales between $20 and $48 billion, but not long ago the Institute of Defense Analysis issued a report which indicated that if supersonic travel were restricted to overwater flights, there would be a market for only 279 planes and the whole project would become an economic disaster.

Even if the SST is initially operated at supersonic speeds only on overwater flights, mounting economic pressures to expand the market for the plane will almost certainly result in overland routes across the United States. Former Transportation Secretary Alan Boyd has said: "I think it will be entirely possible to operate a route over the Plains area and possibly across the Canadian border without discomfort or inconvenience to people on the ground."

The operation of such a route would reduce the flying time between Chicago and San Francisco only about thirty minutes. If supersonic flight on overland routes is not restricted, 150 SST's may be in domestic operation by 1990. Must 50 million people be subjected to perhaps thirty booms a day so that a few can reduce their travel time by thirty minutes?

While the abatement of much of the noise that presently plagues our society is in part a technical problem, both the impetus and the money for solving it must come from the political arena, and the sonic boom problem is entirely political. A quieter society will only be achieved when a concerned public demands a new system of priorities from the politicians.

AIR POLLUTION: A NATIONWIDE SURVEY [9]

As America's air becomes steadily more contaminated, activities across the nation to cope with smog appear to be lagging further and further behind actual needs despite a rising public clamor for improvement.

This is tacitly acknowledged by qualified Federal and state officials. It is reflected in the latest statistics. . . . One Federal official summed up the situation this way:

There has been a lot of progress in the last couple of years. But the overall picture is that so many localities haven't really come to grips with the air pollution problem that people might be appalled if they knew how their welfare was being trifled with.

Air pollution sources are now hurling more than 140 million tons of contaminants into the atmosphere every year, by Federal estimates. Two years ago it was only 130 million tons.

The increase has been caused by many things—more people, more automobiles, more industry, more space heating, little if any reduction in fumes from refuse disposal, control activities that more often than not are inadequate.

The adverse health effects of air pollution are becoming more widely recognized, although specific medical evidence is still fragmentary. As a psychological annoyance, often called an "esthetic" factor, it translates into decreased property values. In damage to crops and other plants, its cost is reckoned in millions of dollars; in damage to structures and materials, in billions.

Highlights of Situation

Federal and state pollution control officials report the following highlights of the current situation.

1. States and localities generally still have penalties for air pollution that are little more than a wrist slap (with fines as low as $10). Enforcement is generally sketchy and weak. And the remedial procedures are so cumbersome that more

[9] From "Air Pollution Grows Despite Rising Public Alarm," by Gladwin Hill, national environmental correspondent. New York *Times.* p 1+. O. 19, '69. © 1969 by The New York Times Company. Reprinted by permission.

and more they are being bypassed by simple lawsuits brought by public officials or citizens.

2. Administration in many places is still muddled. Both the city of Chicago and Cook County have agencies concerned with what is essentially one air basin. A similar situation exists in Houston, Texas. Residents of Cincinnati and many other cities complain about fumes from factories just beyond the city boundaries and thus beyond the reach of city pollution regulations.

3. Although Federal law for two years has required auto makers to provide vehicles with fume control equipment, few states have done anything to assure their effectiveness, after a car has left the factory, by providing for regular inspection of the equipment.

4. Few states have gone as far as to ban open burning and backyard incinerators, although these are significant contributors to air pollution and experts agree that they are outdated as means of waste disposal.

5. Public officials in many places still seem to consider flurries of complaints from citizens preferable to the complaints they might get from instituting effective air quality programs. Industries and other polluters, such as municipalities, still wield great influence, opposing or weakening regulatory laws and "packing" regulatory boards with their own spokesmen.

6. Public resentment over air pollution is growing, as is shown by recurring incidents of picketing and an increasing number of legal actions.

The big Federal program to combat air pollution, under way for several years, is proceeding fairly close to schedule. But Federal auto-fume regulations will not be very productive for nearly a decade—until around 100 million unregulated, older-generation cars have been replaced on the highways.

The part of the Federal effort that deals with stationary pollution sources, like factories, is still largely in an organizational phase, yielding little immediate reduction in fumes.

States, Counties and Cities

The brunt of the responsibility for dealing with stationary-source pollution has, under the basic Federal concept, always rested with the states, counties and cities. And their performance to date, reports from around the country make plain, has been no better than spotty.

The total amount of money budgeted ... [for 1969] by all state, regional and local air pollution control agencies ... [was] $47 million, according to the National Air Pollution Control Administration.

That is less than 25 cents for each person in the country, whereas Federal experts have estimated that 25 cents per capita is a minimal expenditure on the local level alone for effective air pollution control.

The figure of 25 cents compares with a national per capita expenditure of $15 a year to deal with the relatively simple problem of solid waste.

Moreover, nearly half of the expenditure by states and localities—$20.5 million out of $47.3 million—is Federal rather than local money.

Federal Expenditures

The law permits the Federal Government to pay up to 75 per cent of the cost of some regional pollution control activities. Since 1965, the Department of Health, Education, and Welfare has paid out more than $58 million in grants.

Every community has its own distinctive combination of smog sources. But across the nation roughly half of all air pollution appears to come from automobiles and half from stationary sources.

In its effort to cope with stationary-source smog, the Federal Government is interested primarily in fifty-seven metropolitan areas currently being designated as "air quality control regions." The National Air Pollution Control Administration has started promulgating air quality criteria, in specific chemical terms, for those communities.

The respective states are supposed to provide control programs conforming with the criteria. Under a fifteen-month development schedule that went into effect . . . [in February 1969], these programs are due to start materializing in mid-1970, with metropolitan New York and metropolitan Philadelphia as two of the first areas on the list.

Aside from these fifty-seven specified areas, it is up to states and localities to initiate smog control systems. While there have been some conspicuous advances in the last year or two, the national picture is not greatly different from that of three years ago—except for a mounting volume of public protests.

The Rise of Protest

Citizens of Louisville staged a march wearing gas masks, and collected 13,000 signatures on a petition protesting emissions of the Air Reduction Company, which makes acetylene gas from carbide.

The demonstration got results. The local air pollution control board went to court and got an order to require the company to comply with clean air regulations. In August the company completed the replacement of dust-spewing furnaces with $5.2 million worth of electric burners, reducing emissions from 11 tons a day to 100 pounds.

California's impatience with automobile fumes welled up . . . in a spectacular gesture by a respected legislator: The introduction of a bill to ban the conventional internal combustion car engine from California in 1980.

The bill died in committee, but was generally taken as a constructive admonition to automobile manufacturers that California would not accept anything less than a maximum effort in fume reduction.

Los Angeles is still the only metropolis in the country that has virtually cleared its skies of pollution from stationary sources and that has an air pollution control agency generally regarded as large enough and effective.

It has a staff of three hundred and a [1969] budget . . . of $4.6 million. Over the last twenty years, the agency has taken more than 40,000 offenders into court, with a 96 per cent conviction rate and fines totaling more than $1 million. No other city comes close to this tight an administration.

Boston, cited by the Federal Government two years ago as the seventh most smog-afflicted city in the country, only now is getting around to considering—with a three-member staff and a $60,000 budget—control regulations.

Detroit issued 4,100 citations last year, but only 85 offenders were brought to court. Louisville, Kentucky, has issued 769 citations this year, but only rarely, do first-offenders receive any penalty.

Massachusetts authorities, over a recent five-year period, brought only 22 court actions against polluters.

Michigan has issued only 22 cease-and-desist orders since 1965, although several hundred investigations are reported in progress.

An Illinois legislative committee, after a year's investigation, reported this year that the nine-member State Air Pollution Board had been remiss in protecting public health, dilatory in promulgating and enforcing rules, and lax in granting open-burning permits "in virtual disregard of the intent of the law."

Qualified officials of New York's State Air Resources Board say its budget of $2 million and staff of 185 are less than adequate. Some courts make abatement difficult. The operation of an Albany cement plant that showers dust on the surrounding countryside was defended by a judge as important to the regional economy. And in a current case, the issue is whether the stench from an Albany hog farm can be categorized as air pollution.

Slow Improvement

Across the country, there is scattered evidence of improvement.

Kentucky's state air pollution control staff has grown over the last four years from 4 persons to 33. Texas's state agency has grown since 1966 from 3 part-time employees with a budget of $11,000 to 40 full-time employees with a budget of $450,000, and it has obtained fines of as much as $17,500 against industrial polluters.

Chicago's control program has grown in five years from 84 employees with a $770,000 budget to 145 employees with a $1,384,000 budget.

But such advances are still the exception. The generally slow pace of progress can be attributed in part to the complexities of air pollution, which challenge both official administration and public understanding, and to inertia and outright obstruction.

Pennsylvania now has an air pollution control program under way, but for ten years after the nation's worst smog disaster—the suffocation in 1948 of twenty residents of Donora, Pennsylvania, from smelter fumes—the Pennsylvania Legislature annually rejected air pollution control bills.

California's state capital is annually shrouded in haze as stubble is burned by Sacramento Valley rice farmers who are exempt from the air pollution laws.

In New York, farm groups this year maneuvered through the legislature an open-burning exemption that was stopped only by Governor Rockefeller's veto.

Are Polluters In Control?

A classic case of obstruction occurred in Texas, where lobbyists for the state's 1,300 cotton gins in 1967 got them exempted, obtaining a ban on the use of any state funds to regulate their emissions. Only after a two-year legislative struggle was the exemption annulled. ...

On air pollution control boards across the country, it is common practice to allocate several seats to industry, although industry is the most likely candidate for regulation. Colorado's nine-member board, for example, contains two doctors, an engineer, three representatives of the public and three representatives of industry.

A lawyer in Chicago recently filed a citizen's suit against the city alleging that 13 of 27 positions on the smog appeals board and three advisory committees were occupied by representatives of big polluters.

More often than not, inquiries to state and local officials about air pollution law enforcement bring the response in effect: "We prefer to work through persuasion and negotiation and voluntary compliance." Experts regard this as a tip-off that polluters are still in control.

"Reasonable discussion with polluters about remedial steps is important," says Louis Fuller, director of the Los Angeles County control agency. "But there has to be the knowledge that if they don't shape up, they're going to land in court as sure as God made little apples."

The Future Outlook

What is the outlook for cleaner air?

Some observers, particularly among scientists and environmentalists, are pessimistic that the nation will [not] begin to meet the problem of air pollution until, perhaps, it is too late.

"We are a crisis-oriented society," one said. "We react only to emergencies. And we can't wait until every city in the country has had an emergency like Donora, Pennsylvania, or New York's and Los Angeles's sieges of smog."

Air pollution experts, with a shorter-range focus on developments, seem more optimistic. They note that there are now approximately two hundred state, regional and local air pollution agencies where a decade ago there were almost none; that expenditures have gone virtually from zero to their current level in that time; that there has been an immense amount of scientific and technical knowledge about smog developed in that short period, and that great strides have been made in such important collateral areas as the training of personnel in air pollution control, in which most large universities and colleges now have courses. . . .

Air pollution experts say the pace of progress depends largely on how much pressure the public eventually brings on politicians and administrators.

Solving air pollution is a lot more complicated than putting a man on the moon [one official observed], but there's one vital factor in both undertakings: A majority of the people have to be determined that the job is worth doing, and that it shall be done.

III. RESCUING OUR WATER RESOURCES

EDITOR'S INTRODUCTION

The pollution of our rivers has become a national scandal
which is now being tackled with vigor although with limited
resources. And we debate whether Lake Erie is actually dying. At the same time a disastrous oil leak off the coast of
Santa Barbara, California, alerts us anew to the pollution of
our ocean resources.

These topics are dealt with first by an article from
Reader's Digest and two somewhat contrasting views of just
how endangered are Lake Erie and the other Great Lakes.
Oil pollution of the off-shore ocean waters and on the high
seas is next surveyed by an authority on ecology. Because
much of the pollution of our waterways arises from wastes
unloaded by industrial plants, a statement from the president of E. I. du Pont de Nemours & Company, Charles B.
McCoy, is included as the final selection in the section, indicating industry's concern about water pollution abatement.

AMERICA'S POLLUTED WATERWAYS [1]

We seem to have turned the corner—just!—on river pollution. There's nothing glorious yet to report, only small gains:
perhaps the crabs are back in the lower reaches of the river;
swimming is allowed again at some spot that used to be polluted; the chemical plant upriver has stopped killing fish. It
isn't much, but it is the difference between up and down.
And in the next couple of years, as more sources of pollution
dry up, your local river should get noticeably better. Toward

[1] From "The Great American River Cleanup," by Wolfgang Langewiesche,
roving editor, free-lance writer and author of *I'll Take the High Road. Reader's
Digest.* 94:213+. My. '69. Reprinted with permission from the May 1969
Reader's Digest. Copyright 1969 by The Reader's Digest Assn., Inc.

1980 we should see a glorious clearing of our rivers, followed in the nineties by a clearing of the lakes.

The great nationwide cleanup began in 1965. It started quietly, for a peculiar reason: everybody was for it. First, Congress passed the Water Quality Act of 1965 (which established the Federal Water Pollution Control Administration), and then the Clean Water Restoration Act of 1966. These two laws, passed without a dissenting vote, put the power and the money of the Federal Government behind that of the states and cities—to help them build sewage plants. Because that's what it takes: thousands of big, factory-like plants which clean the water before it goes back into the river.

Then why so slow? Why talk of 1980? Because it takes years of persistence to get such plants built—to get the decision through the city council, get the land, fight the lawsuits, float the bonds. Whether we persist or not will depend largely on whether people understand what has been done, what's being done, what *can* be done.

How bad is the mess? It's bad, all right. Most people don't realize how grim it is. . . . It was all right to dump our organic dirt into the rivers as long as the volume was small. Water has a miraculous ability to clean itself; microbes take dirt apart until it isn't dirty anymore. But these microbes need oxygen—the same oxygen, dissolved in the water, that lets fish breathe. If you put too much organic matter into a river, it draws out all the oxygen, the beneficial microbes can't live, and the river loses its power of self-purification. Bubbles of gas rise from the bottom, scum forms at the water's edge, the water is gray and putrid. The river becomes, in effect, a septic tank, like a stretch of the majestic Hudson below Albany, which contains nothing but sludge-worms and a type of eel that lives on human excrement.

Lakes are in trouble in a different way. Main fact: practically any substance that we put into a lake stays there, almost forever. Right now, nearly half of all public bathing beaches on the U.S. side of Lake Erie are unsafe for swimming. Near Cleveland, the colon bacillus (sign of human excrement) often occurs in concentrations one hundred times what is considered safe for swimming.

Detergents, too, are a problem. Some years ago, it looked as if all our lakes and rivers were soon going to be covered with foam. Then the detergent manufacturers changed their formulas, greatly reducing the foaming. But the detergents still contain phosphorus, and that is a plant food. Algae are plants; ergo, detergents make algae grow. Algae make water taste and smell unpleasant; and when they die, *their* decomposition requires oxygen. In this way, detergents draw down the oxygen reserves of a lake, even one as large as Lake Erie. At times, large stretches of Erie are now covered with algae "bloom," a green scum. Often, masses of rotting algae are swept on the beaches, and the slime and stench are almost intolerable. Lake Erie may be on its way to turning into a bog. Almost all our lakes could face the same fate. . . . In rivers, the phosphorus problem is less serious because the water reaches the sea before all the fertilizer in it has been taken up by algae.

Recent Antipollution Legislation

Since 1965, pollution of interstate streams has been a Federal matter. The new setup gives the states three new reasons to enforce their laws: (1) the threat of Federal action makes state officials more eager to act, and makes the polluter more ready to comply; (2) the availability of Federal aid makes it more *practical* for the state to enforce or accomplish nonpollution; (3) the nationwide character of the drive has nullified the once valid excuse: "If I take on this expense, I'll be noncompetitive with other cities (or companies) which do not have such expenses."

Under the Water Quality Act, each state is invited to set its own standards of water purity and to enforce these standards—or else the Federal Government will. Naturally, all states have chosen to run their own show.

Many of them have passed tough new clean-water laws, and strengthened their enforcement agencies. Some have also appropriated a lot of money with which to help municipalities build sewage-treatment plants. New York State voters, for instance, have passed a billion-dollar bond issue; Michigan, $285 million; Massachusetts, $150 million; Pennsylvania; $100 million; Washington, $25 million. The Federal Government also chips in: $3-$5 billion has been authorized for the cities since 1967. The formula is complicated, but typically the city, state and Federal shares are 40-30-30.

Meanwhile, in years of effort, Federal researchers have explored our rivers and lakes, and cataloged the sources of pollution, naming names. You should see those lists: big cities, small cities, factories, railroads, a famous university, Uncle Sam himself. And public knowledge of these facts has great force. A company knowingly dumps hundreds of gallons of oil into a river every day. Confronted with the facts, called upon to clean up, the company dares not risk public censure or a bad press. What really can it say but "Yes, sir"?

In fact, industry seems especially willing to cooperate, now that the law hitches up industries and cities in a system of mutual self-interest. For the first time, as I clean water for other people, I know that other people are cleaning water for me. As I have to add to my cost of production, I know that my competitors have to do the same. This makes all the difference.

The Technology of Antipollution

There are three stages of cleaning sewage water. "Primary" treatment is mechanical. A sort of sieve takes out the gross impurities. Then the water is allowed to stand in settling basins; more dirt sinks to the bottom and can be drained off. This takes out about one third of the pollution load.

Secondary treatment is biological. It imitates the natural self-cleaning of rivers: microbes take the dirt apart. To grow more microbes faster, you blow air bubbles through the dirty water, or in some other way give it lots of contact with air; you also "inoculate" the incoming sewage by mixing it with a sludge which is already teeming with these microbes. This sort of treatment does in hours what the natural river would do in days. Careful secondary treatment, followed by chlorination to kill disease germs, reduces the pollution load by 90 per cent.

But even after secondary treatment, the effluent still contains organic particles and all of the salts, acids, dyes, phenols, insecticides, medicines, fertilizers, algae-growing phosphorus and other chemicals we have put into it. It is already clear that, as our cities and industries grow (while our rivers do not), we shall have to go one step further—and give sewage a tertiary treatment that cleans the water all the way, for use a second time. This is not the practice now; but Federal planners think it will have to come, or our civilization *will* run out of water. Both private industry and the Federal Government are sponsoring research in third-stage cleaning. Right now, the aim is merely to make secondary treatment, plus chlorination, a universal practice. By 1980 or so, *no* sewage is to reach any American river that has not had this amount of cleaning. It will be a huge job.

One source of pollution that must be corrected is the so-called combined sewer. In the older sections of cities, water from streets and roofs drains directly into the sewers. Every time it rains, a big flood comes down the sewer system and goes through the overflow bypass directly into the river, flushing a load of raw sewage along with it. To stop it is an urgent task. But how? To construct separate storm sewers *now* in all cities would cost perhaps $49 billion. The digging up of downtown streets would lead to intolerable traffic snarls.

One solution could be a reservoir where dirty floodwater can be held for a day or so, until it can be run through the treatment plant. But where do you put such a reservoir? Now, under the new laws, the Federal Government is helping to find a solution. Chicago, given a Federal grant of $1.5

million, is digging a holding basin in the form of a tunnel 200 feet under the city, four miles long, between 12 and 17 feet in diameter. If it works, cities may build hundreds of miles of such tunnels.

Also with Federal aid, Washington, D.C., Sandusky, Ohio, and Cambridge, Maryland, have just had installed a different and experimental type of reservoir. It is *in* the river, under water. It consists of huge bags of strong, watertight fabric. Normally they are empty and lie in loose folds on the river bottom. When storm water overloads the combined sewer, the excess flow is channeled into the bags. They then swell up like blimps—*under* water, *in* the river, with each bag holding 100,000 to 200,000 gallons of dirty water right there. After a day or so, the dirty water is pumped out to the treatment plant, and the blimps shrink again to almost nothing. You can see the advantages: no extra space required, no real estate, no dam, no earth moving.

Who pays for all this? You and I do, of course. Where the various governments build the treatment plants, we'll pay for them in taxes. Where industries have to build them, we'll pay for them in slightly higher-priced products. Therefore it really makes little difference who builds them. The important thing is to get them built.

LAKE ERIE: A DYING LAKE? [2]

Man is destroying Lake Erie [says the report from the Federal Water Pollution Control Administration]. Although the accelerating destruction process has been inadvertent, it is as positive as if he had put all his energies into devising and implementing the means. After two generations the process has gained a momentum which now requires a monumental effort to retard. The effort must not only be basinwide and highly coordinated; it must be immediate. Every moment lost in allowing the destruction to continue will require a longer, more difficult, and more expensive corrective action.

    [2] From "Life on a Dying Lake," by Peter Schrag, editor-at-large. *Saturday Review.* 52:19-21+. S. 20, '69. Reprinted by permission. Copyright 1969 Saturday Review, Inc.

Prosaic language from Washington: eutrophication, secondary treatment, nutrient removal, algal blooms, biological oxygen demand. There is little romance in a sewage plant, and none in the technicalities of oxygen depletion, thermal stratification, or discharge of organic wastes. But the destruction of a lake is not merely a technical or a political problem. To think of it is to think of all America, of our love-hate relationship with our technology, about our ambivalence about who we are and what we are, about the Hudson and the Missouri, about the Santa Barbara Channel and nuclear bombs, about defoliation in Vietnam and DDT-poisoned fish in Michigan—about all the things we value, often in contradiction—in our past and our future. . . .

Some 13 million people live in the basin of this lake, 90 per cent of them on the American side, the rest in Ontario, the polluters and the polluted, perpetrators and victims, all of them dependent on a body of water that, according to the best evidence, is not yet dead but in danger. They drink its water, swim on its beaches, eat its fish, and sail from its harbors. At the same time, they, their cities, and their factories each day dump, leak, pipe, or drop into the lake several hundred million pounds of sewage, chemicals, oil, and detergents fouling beaches, killing wildlife, and imperiling the water itself. Sometimes you can smell and taste it as it comes out of the tap, sometimes you can see it on the beaches and often in the rivers—the Maumee, the Auglaize, the Ottawa—but most significantly, you fear, not what already exists, but what might—and could happen—if the process continues. . . .

Everything contributes to, and suffers from, the condition of the lake: people in five states and a Canadian province—hundreds of towns and cities from Toledo to Buffalo: Akron, Erie, Cleveland, Lorain, Conneaut, Ashtabula. The Federal Government has identified 360 sources of industrial waste—power plants, steel mills, chemical companies, food processors, rubber companies. During every heavy rain, flooding sewers and silt spill into the lake, and even in normal periods silt and fertilizers and pesticides drain into its tributaries. But the greatest polluters may be the city sewage systems themselves.

The Federal Government has estimated that with existing treatment facilities, the cities along the lake discharge effluent equal, in its composition and effects on the lake, to the raw sewage from a population of 4.7 million people. Some cities are providing secondary treatment, some primary, some none at all. Lake Erie has been called a huge cesspool, an appellation that has at least marginal accuracy. What is absolutely accurate is the statement that in the past fifty years pollution has substantially altered the ecology of the lake, and that it has made the lake far older than its years.

The Process of Eutrophication

The word, among the scientists, is eutrophication—the process of aging. All lakes grow old as they collect runoff and materials from the surrounding shores. Over thousands of years they eventually accumulate enough silt from erosion and organic materials to turn them into marshes and, finally, into dry land. In Lake Erie man has accelerated that process with his wastes and sewage. An excess of nutrients, primarily phosphates and nitrates, has produced great growths of algae in the water and impaired the oxygen supply, especially in the deeper water during the summer—and especially at the western end, which is hit hardest by the excrement from Detroit. (Biological degrading of the nutrients requires oxygen; when the nutrients are too heavy the oxygen becomes depleted.)

Mayflies, which once grew in huge numbers in the western, the shallowest, end of the lake, and which provided a food supply for fish—cisco, blue pike, walleye, and other species—have declined; the water has been taken over by sheepshead, carp, and other types that are tolerant of low-oxygen conditions and whose eggs can survive the accumulation of sediments at the bottom. Some species that have surmounted changes in food supply and depleted oxygen now take longer to reach maturity. (The total volume of fish caught in the lake each year is as large as ever, but the catch is worth only half of what it was ten years ago; most of the fishing is now done by Canadians.)

On occasion there have been duck kills, flights of birds which have landed on oily water and never flew again, either (it is assumed) because the oil destroyed the birds' natural protection against the water, or because they were poisoned. (There has been some serious talk in recent years about oil drilling in the lake. So far the derricks of the Canadian Pacific Oil and Gas Company, which have been erected on the Ontario side of the lake, are producing only natural gas.) There is also a possibility that the algae, under certain conditions, can manufacture their own poisons, endangering wild life—and possibly human life.

Because the lake is relatively shallow, there is hope that once the rate of pollution is retarded (hopefully, but not certainly, through improved sewage treatment), the lake, with proper oxygen circulation, can recover, spilling its wastes into Lake Ontario and, ultimately, into the Atlantic. The certainty of that recovery and the effectiveness of the measures now being planned (which, among other things, include the removal of phosphates before effluent is discharged into the lake) are still matters of debate—and of time. What is not a matter of debate is that in the past 50 years, Lake Erie has aged 15,000 years.

Barry Commoner, a Washington University (St. Louis) biologist, who has long been concerned with the abuses of technology, writes:

The lake is threatened with death. . . . Since the area was first settled, Lake Erie has been increasingly burdened with organic wastes and with inorganic nutrients that the lake's algae convert to organic materials. These organic materials would long ago have asphyxiated most of the lake's living things had it not been for the peculiar power of Iron III [an iron compound called ferric iron] to form insoluble complexes with the materials of the bottom mud. The protective skin of Iron III has held the enormous accumulation of potential oxygen-demanding material in the muddy bottom of the lake. But this protective skin can remain intact only so long as there is sufficient oxygen present in the water over the mud. For many years this was so, and the layer of Iron III held the accumulating mud materials out of the lake water. But a serious oxygen depletion now occurs in the summer months. As a result, the protective layer of Iron III has begun to break down—exposing the lake to heavy impact of the accumulated algal nutrient long stored in the mud. If the process continues, we may face a sudden biological cataclysm that will exhaust, for a time, most of the oxygen in the greater part of the lake water. Such a catastrophe would make the lake's present difficulties seem slight by comparison.

The fear is that under existing conditions, Erie could, without warning, turn into a huge swamp. Among the officials of the Federal Water Pollution Control Administration (FWPCA), which is charged with enforcing pollution control measures, Commoner is regarded as a prophet of gloom, a false Cassandra who is trying to frighten people. Nonetheless, FWPCA paraphrased Commoner's statement in its own report on the lake. "Some of that," said one FWPCA official, "was a little exaggerated. We know that the Iron III tends to break down and to release nutrients from the bottom, but there hasn't been any cataclysm, and there's not going to be one."

And yet, perhaps, that's not the issue—shouldn't be the issue. The trouble with conservation is that it has always been a matter of calamities and cataclysms. In the confusion of state, local, and Federal antipollution responsibilities, there is always a large measure of sympathy for the company or the city that has to spend money for better treatment facilities, for the corporate taxpayer who might move somewhere else, for the time it takes, for the problems involved. The questions are thus always questions of resources, of priorities, of urgency and time. How much are fish worth? What's the value of a duck? What is the relationship between defoliants in Vietnam (or the price of automobiles in Detroit) and an acid discharge on the Cuyahoga or the Maumee? . . .

Government Controls Involved

Under the club of Federal authority, all the states in the lake region—Indiana, Ohio, Michigan, New York, and Pennsylvania—have committed themselves to upgrading their municipal waste-treatment facilities to the point where 80 per cent of all phosphates are removed from sewage effluent before it is discharged into the lake. (Some cities are already behind schedule and have received extensions.) Detroit and Cleveland, among others, are building new plants and collection facilities, using local, state, and a little Federal money. At the same time, their officers are angry at the paltry Federal contribution. While Detroit is scheduled to spend $159 million and Cleveland has voted its $100 million bond issue for better treatment and collection, the Federal Government spends barely more than $200 million a year on pollution research and development for the entire nation. "The Federal people are the biggest hypocrites in the bunch," said a Detroit official. "They go around the country making speeches. Maybe if they made as much noise about getting us more money as they do about dirt, we'd be able to move a little faster." The reply from Washington: "The people who are polluting are responsible."

So far, the lake has been unaffected, and there is doubt that even after the scheduled projects are completed they will be sufficient. In New York State, a Health Department advisory committee of scientists was asked the question: Will phosphate removal retard eutrophication in Lake Erie? The answer, in simple words: Don't expect too much. Nonetheless, FWPCA has committed itself to the process as a necessary first step: phosphates, which come largely from detergents, say the FWPCA technicians, are essential to the growth of algae and plankton, so (because it is relatively easy) phosphates will be removed. No one has yet figured out what to do with the phosphates once they are precipitated out. They will be trucked to . . . where? (Nor is it certain that nitrates, which flood into the lake from agricultural fertilizers, and other sources, are not major factors in eutrophication.) . . .

The FWPCA has estimated that it will cost $1.1 billion in pollution control projects to arrest the process of eutrophication in the next twenty years. Some critics believe the figure is far too low, and a few believe that the job is already impossible, that the lake may already be too far gone.

CONTROLLING THE GREAT LAKES POLLUTION [3]

The intent of our national policy to upgrade water resources is admirable, but I am most concerned about its implementation. Emotional and exaggerated views of water pollution are common. In such a mental environment it is often difficult to establish realistic abatement needs, costs, benefits, and priorities. I am fearful that we will be spending a great deal of money for nebulous results unless we put the problem in perspective and determine how to have our pollution control dollar obtain the best results.

Before we say that water pollution now constitutes a "crisis condition," we must recognize that there has never been a time in recorded history when some aspect of the earth's water has not been a problem to man, who has always been threatened by floods, droughts, or pollution near population centers. . .

We have made extraordinary progress in pollution abatement from the viewpoint of human health. Never in history was so much accomplished by so few in so short a time as in the reduction in waterborne disease in the late nineteenth and twentieth centuries. Today in the United States waterborne disease is most unusual; the quality of water supplies in cities has never been equal to its present con-

[3] From "Outwitting the Patient Assassin: The Human Use of Lake Pollution," by Harold B. Gotaas, a civil and sanitary engineer and dean of the Technological Institute of Northwestern University. *Bulletin of the Atomic Scientists.* 25:8-10. My. '69. Reprinted by permission of Science and Public Affairs (*Bulletin of the Atomic Scientists*). Copyright © 1969 by the Educational Foundation for Nuclear Science.

dition. This brief history is worth recalling because some recent public statements have caused general unease by their seeming indications that a good job has not been done in safeguarding the health of the people from water pollution. Our guardians (national, state, and local) of man's water have done an outstanding job of protecting our health, and society should not be led to believe that they have been negligent of their responsibilities or that our potable water supplies are not satisfactory.

The water pollution problems today are not directly associated with health and the spread of disease; they center on the fish and wildlife of the country, on recreational uses of natural resources, on the chemical and biological quality of the waters, and on the desire for a more satisfactory environment. For many years there has been a reduction in the proportion of man's wastes disposed into water. But the total amount and concentration of wastes produced in some areas has been increasing more rapidly than the increases in the proportions removed by treatment. We need to reduce the amount of wastes emptied into our fresh waters. The problem is to accomplish this efficiently and with a priority schedule which will yield greatest benefits in relation to costs.

The Problem of the Great Lakes

The proper approach to the problem is the realistic one. An example of the unproductive and exaggerated view of the water pollution problem is the often repeated remark that Lake Erie is dead and beyond recovery. The fact is that Lake Erie is far from dead and can be cleaned up by removing the severe pollution at many points along the shores. It is improbable that Lake Erie can be returned to its condition of one hundred years ago, but it is also doubtful that the benefits of that degree of restoration would be worth the costs when compared with other needs for pleasant living. The challenge is to look realistically and logically at the problems. The "Save Our Lake" publicity assumes that Lake Michigan is a rapidly dying lake. It is obvious that the serious pollution at the south end of the lake and at other points should be cleaned up, but except for these points the lake is healthy. The average concentration of nutrients is not high in Lake Michigan or in Lake Superior. I am very dubious about the efficacy of the present emphasis on excessive removal of municipal waste nutrients as a means of reviving the Great Lakes.

The pollution problem in the Great Lakes must be subjected to realistic analysis before any such steps are taken. We have very limited information on increases in algae growth except at points of very high pollution in shallow waters. Besides, other factors are as important to algae growth as pollution. Further nutrient relationships and costs versus benefits studies should be undertaken for guidance in building expensive facilities on a large scale for the purpose of algae control. Even if all the phosphorus were removed from waste, there is probably enough phosphorus and nitrogen in runoff from land to supply the needs for algae growth at present usual concentrations in large bodies of water. Removing excessive pollution from places such as the south end of Lake Michigan would no doubt satisfactorily reduce the algae growth. Green Bay presents another problem with respect to algae since it grew high concentrations before the area was highly populated. Perhaps in a number of small lakes it makes sense to reduce the nutrient levels as a means of algae control.

Algae, of course, are a significant element in the food chain of a body of water. They utilize nutrients in the water to grow, and are fed upon by higher forms of biological life, consumed, in turn, by fish. As with any plant, algae give off oxygen when exposed to sunlight. The oxygen then stimulates bacteria which help assimilate organic pollution. I have actually seen algae supersaturate water with oxygen so that it bubbled off the surface. Algae then can be beneficial in cleaning up water under proper conditions, particularly where the algae are consumed by other forms of life. The problem comes, though, when the algae growths get out of hand. As the plants die they contribute to the organic waste load which consumes oxygen and recycles the nutrients such as phosphorus and nitrogen. The need is to keep a proper biological balance in a water body.

Conceivably, algae could be harvested to prevent its contributing to the organic waste load. The varieties of algae range from one-celled plants to the large, rooted water weeds often seen around shorelines. Our studies have shown that large algae yields consisting of 45 per cent to 55 per cent protein could be produced. By contrast, alfalfa has only about 21 per cent protein and it sells for about $40 per ton. It is clear that algae has great potential as a source of food. The basic concept of algae harvesting has real merit and should be best accomplished in special ponds prior to emptying effluents into lakes.

But there are a number of problems in the harvesting of it. First of all, treating wastes and nutrient removal by algae requires a lot more space than is necessary for usual waste treatment processes. Then, in our work with unicellular algae, we had trouble filtering it out of the water: the little cells were like balloons and would fill in the filter openings. We need to find better techniques and to develop a type of algae that can be harvested more easily.

Maintaining a Biological Balance

The biological balance in large bodies of water has been affected, primarily, not by pollution but by overfishing and the effects of such predators as the lamprey and the recent invasion of alewives. The best way to get nutrients out of the Great Lakes is to seed them with desirable fish to establish the food chain on a better basis. For example, a twenty-pound coho salmon or other desirable fish can eat a lot of alewives or zooplankton in the biological life chain, which in turn consume nutrients. If the lakes are well stocked with the coho and other desirable fish, and good commercial sport fishing is reestablished, great quantities of nutrients will be removed with every ton of fish. This seems the more direct approach to the problem of nutrient removal—the cost would be considerably less, and the goals of pollution control and better fishing would be furthered.

Some fish can do well even in a lake as polluted as Lake Erie, a relatively shallow lake in which dead algae and organic matter from wastes settle to the bottom in areas of excess pollution. There the material is decomposed with an accompanying reduction in the dissolved oxygen. When fish seek colder water near the bottom during warmer weather, they may die because of too little available oxygen. There are two avenues to the solution of this problem. First, the excessive pollutants must be kept out of the lake. Second, desirable fish which are more temperature and oxygen tolerant should be seeded in the lake. As nutrients are removed by the harvest of these fish in recreational and commercial fishing, the nutrient load in the lake will be further reduced. A major reduction of the pollution emptied into the lake, the removal of nutrients by fish, and the carrying out of some of the present nutrients by the flowing through of water (in its course to the ocean) will eventually restore the lake quality to a desirable level.

A lake can be thought of as an aquarium. If toxic materials are not added to the water it would be possible to establish a desirable biological balance which would permit the growth and removal of fish for food needs as well as for sport. Nutrients are needed to support a desirable fish population.

Some fish have considerable adaptability to lower oxygen levels for short periods when migrating. Salmon have been observed to withstand serious harm in water having three to four parts per million of oxygen when migrating, but could not spend a lifetime in waters of low concentration. It would seem, therefore, that the dissolved oxygen standards set to maintain the production of fish are somewhat arbitrary. We have a lot to learn about the relationship of fish to their environment; the oxygen levels for fish propagation and survival are based on very limited information. In a population of any type of fish, some are more tolerant than others and there are laboratory indications that increased tolerance may take place. So there is some prospect of developing more resistant strains of desirable fish, which would certainly aid in achieving the goal while other pollution control measures are becoming effective.

Water Quality Standards

Ideally, of course, it would be better to raise the quality of the water than to raise the tolerance of the fish. But we have to be practical. The Water Quality Act of 1965 and the Clean Waters Restoration Act of 1966 have been important steps toward solving some of the water pollution problems. Water quality standards have now been set by all of the states. Certain standards may be found to be too high and unrealistic relative to costs and benefits, some vague, some too low. But, no doubt, most of the quality standards are sound, and it is desirable that we have them even though we find later that some of them are inappropriate as to cost, benefits, and time priorities. For example, in a water channel necessary for commercial transportation and waste carriage, are the benefits worth the costs of also providing for water recreation and quality fishing? Is the benefit worth the cost of maintaining five to six parts per million of oxygen for quality game fish in some multiple-use waters? Is it worth the cost to maintain high dissolved oxygen concentrations in waste outfalls subject to later diffusion? Is it worth the cost to limit waste concentrations discharged well out into the ocean where the water already has high concentrations of salts?

Environmental Control in Perspective

One important function of our water resources is the assimilation of wastes which cannot be economically removed. I doubt that we could afford to keep everything out of our water sources—and even if we could, whether it would be worth it. After all, as long as people carry on their activities there will be wastes, some fraction of which must inevitably go into the air and water resources. The problem is to reduce continually that fraction of the total wastes which must go into the air and water, in order to maintain an environmental quality satisfactory for healthful and pleasant living. In some parts of the country, needs dictate greater emphasis on air pollution control, despite the greater publicity on water pollution control.

There is a range of levels of environmental quality. Some are based on health and disaster control; some related to psychological depressiveness, sensory, and individual performance conditions; some related to comfort, recreation, scenic enjoyment, water sports, fish and wildlife, boating, odors, and unsightliness; and others related to damage to crops, materials, and facilities. A question in pollution control at any point in time is: "How much of the benefits in health, comfort and happiness associated with pollution control are we willing to pay for as related to other desires and social needs, such as housing, education, law enforcement, etc.?" The public should expect maximum return for the money spent—the funds come from the people and they should have the best information possible on cost versus benefits to help decide how their money should be spent. Evaluation of incremental changes in our environment beyond those necessary for disaster and illness control are necessary to determine the most effective improvement of our environment.

A characteristic which has set man apart has been his ability to control his environment. I have little doubt but that he will consider the elements necessary for pleasant and healthful living for his and future generations and will manage his environment to provide for his needs.

OIL POLLUTION OF THE OCEANS [4]

Traffic is picking up in the Northwest Passage. The development of northern oil reserves is the lure to the formidable, ice-clogged straits between the North American continent and the permanent Arctic ice pack. The risk in that unreliable seaway which has so long resisted commercial penetration is paralleled by worldwide risk of oil pollution as oilmen reach out with ever larger tankers and more complex equipment to tap remote reserves. The chances taken in the Northwest Passage symbolize the unrelenting search for new sources of oil to meet world consumption (expected to reach 76 million barrels by 1975, more than twice the amount in 1967).

Canadian federal government officials watch the activities with as much concern about Canada's uncertain territorial rights in the region as about the possibility of oil pollution. The latter problem, however, was dramatized toward the end of August when a supply ship and barges on the way to one drilling station were trapped in the ice with possible loss of 400,000 gallons of fuel oil. Shortly afterward, the 950-foot converted tanker S.S. Manhattan came along with an icebreaker escort, crunching through the passageway at a record pace, to test the feasibility of a route to Prudhoe Bay, Alaska, near the oil-rich Alaskan North Slope. Despite the successful outcome of the Manhattan's voyage, the shifting ice floes will remain treacherous obstacles to general shipping.

The pollution danger that parallels the all-out drive for oil is summarized in the following items:

1. Shipping and port activities release at least one million tons of crude oil into the sea each year; this, plus oil spilled from shore installations, offshore drilling operations, and other sources, may be comparable to the entire production of hydrocarbons by plants and animals in the ocean.

[4] From "The Black Tide," by Julian McCaull, program coordinator of the Center for the Biology of Natural Systems, Washington University, St. Louis, Mo. *Environment*. 11:2-16. N. '69. Copyright 1969 *Environment*. Reprinted by permission.

2. Additional volumes of petroleum products find their way into the sea from bilges and fuel tanks of oil-burning ships, from engine compartments of pleasure crafts, from sunken ships, and from shore activities.

3. Although the short-term biological effects of crude oil appear to be limited—except for the destruction of water-fowl—chronic pollution poses a threat to marine life, the fishing industry, recreation, and the habitats of animals and plants in the tidal zone and along the shore.

4. The tar-like asphaltic residue from crude oil stains vast regions of the sea, particularly in the Atlantic. The unprecedented scale of this change in the marine environment leads to fears of unforeseen consequences.

5. Some of the most beautiful and popular beaches in the world have been invaded by sheets of crude oil in the past few years that have marred natural beauty and sent their acrid stench miles inland.

6. Fuel oil, far more toxic than crude, escapes into the ocean in large quantities that devastate plant and animal life.

7. Methods to counteract oil spills are inadequate and, in the case of certain dispersants, cause more damage to marine life than the oil itself.

Scope of Pollution

As might be expected, most individual pollution crises stem from tanker mishaps. The increase in oil pollution from this source is consistent with the generally rising curve of tanker tonnage lost at sea over the past twenty years. The loss totaled about 200,000 tons in 1948, rose to about 430,000 in 1960, then pushed up to more than 550,000 in 1963. A sharp rise in lost tonnage and in resultant oil pollution occurs after the loss of one large tanker such as the Torrey Canyon, which carried 118,000 tons of crude oil at the time of its grounding on the Seven Stones reef, fifteen miles west of Land's End, England, in 1967. Furthermore, although the ship was one of the ten largest in the world three years ago, its size is run-of-the-mill in comparison with the new supertankers now under construction. Nearly 200 tankers of more than 200,000 tons deadweight—a measure preferred by oilmen as an indication of cargo capacity —have been ordered by shipping companies in recent years. Ships of 500,000 tons deadweight are being designed, and one of a million tons deadweight is thought possible by some shipbuilders. The sobering aspect of the trend toward sea giants is that the loss of one 300,000-ton tanker, several of which are now in service, would equal the total tonnage of all tankers lost at sea ten years ago.

The situation is made more serious by potential crowding in the shipping lanes brought on by increases in the size of the world's fleets. The number of tankers at sea rose from 2,500 in 1955 to 3,600 in 1966; by 1983, the number will be an estimated 4,300, or 700 more than in 1966. In addition, the overall world fleet of tankers, bulk carriers, and freighters is expected to grow from a total of 17,369 in 1966 to 21,468 in 1983.

The risk posed by the heavy traffic and heavy ships is summarized by British experts who prepared the *Report of the Committee of Scientists on the Scientific and Technological Aspects of the Torrey Canyon Disaster:*

The risk of accident is a very real one. In the three years preceding the wreck of the Torrey Canyon, 91 tankers were stranded in various parts of the world, while 238 were involved in collisions either with tankers or other vessels. Over the world at large, tankers have thus been involved in potentially serious accidents on an average of about twice a week for the past three years (prior to 1967). Sixteen of the 329 ships which were concerned became total losses; in 9 of the collisions fire broke out in one or both ships; and in 39 cases cargo spillage or leakage occurred.

Further data is provided by the American Bureau of Shipping, New York City. During the past ten years, 488 American tankers of 30,000 tons deadweight or more have been registered with the bureau. The 488 tankers have been involved in 553 collisions, 17 underwater collisions with submerged objects, and 3 damaging collisions with ice. When asked about the incongruity of more collisions than ships, an official at the bureau replied that some ships had as many as three or four collisions during the ten-year period, while others had none. Overall, oil pollution was a possibility in 43 of the accidents.

The largest number of accidents occur close to shore or in ports, areas that frequently are of greatest economic, nutritional, and esthetic importance to mankind. The trend is clear in a breakdown of location of the 570 collisions and underwater strikings recorded for the 488 American tankers. A total of 472, or 83 per cent, of the incidents occurred while the ships were in or entering port; only 65 took place at sea.

A related development is that many large ports will be dredged or otherwise redesigned to receive supertankers, thus increasing the potential threat from pollution. . . .

A different approach is to establish special terminal facilities for the supertankers outside normal ports. . . .

In addition to accidental spills at sea and in port, voluminous amounts of crude oil are left in the wakes of tankers that discharge oily ballast and tank residues, despite increased legal, political, and competitive pressures against such practices. About 500,000 tons of oil go overboard annually in ballast and bilge water, estimate Graham Brockis and Ray Beynon of the British Petroleum Company in the January 25, 1968, issue of *New Scientist*. Before recent operational changes aboard tankers in some of the major shipping groups to conserve such oily waste, the figure was about 1.5 million tons, the authors estimate. A motivating factor in the reduction is introduction of international standards such as those established by the International Convention for the Prevention of Pollution of the Sea by Oil. The 1954 agreement aims at elimination of dumping along coastal areas and limitation of discharges at sea, but the treaty is flawed by lack of international sanctions. Another incentive to keep the oil on board, of course, is the economic advantage of getting the precious cargo to terminals with minimum losses in transit.

Pollution from shipping and port operations is only part of the problem. Offshore drilling rigs make a contribution, as was dramatized by the Santa Barbara episode. The number of wells drilled annually off the continental United States rose from 500 in 1961 to about 1,100 in 1967, and exploration is underway or planned in waters off 50 countries of the world. Pollution arises from blowouts similar to that in the Santa Barbara Channel, the dumping of oil-based drilling muds and oil-soaked material brought up from the drill holes, and oil losses during production, storage, or pipeline transportation.

The numerous sources of pollution on and under the sea are supplemented by those on shore. As an indication of the scope of that input, the United States Army Corps of Engineers estimated that 40 per cent of two thousand oil spills in the U.S. waters during 1966 were from land-based facilities.

The visible scope of oil pollution was illustrated by Dr. Max Blumer, senior scientist, Department of Chemistry, Woods Hole Oceanographic Institution, at a Boston symposium on oil pollution held . . . [in May 1969]. The meeting was cosponsored by the Institution and the Massachusetts Institute of Technology.

To make his point, Dr. Blumer quoted from the record of a research ship from Woods Hole that towed a special net in the Sargasso Sea to collect certain marine organisms:

> The tows, over a distance of 630 miles, brought up oil tar lumps inevitably during every tow up to three inches in diameter. After twenty-four hours of towing, the mesh became so encrusted with oil that it was necessary to clean the net with solvents. It was estimated that there was three times as much tar-like material as sargasso weed in the nets.

Commented the scientist: "Oil pollution is not only on the shores, where it is very evident, but it is spreading worldwide."

Biological Effects

The oceanwide spread of oil raises the question of biological damage to the marine environment. Unfortunately, scientific data are insufficient, particularly about the long-term effects of major oil spills and chronic pollution.

The situation is complicated by introduction of oil into a complex environment with interdependent food chains and intricate systems of reproduction. Furthermore, the pollution poses biological threats on the high sea that differ in certain respects from those near shore or in ports. At sea, the potential effects on fish, waterfowl, and mammals have received the most publicity since the Torrey Canyon and Santa Barbara episodes, but the most serious long-term hazard may be to tiny organisms such as phytoplankton, one-cell plants that float in countless millions in the upper layers of the seawater and provide food for minute planktonic animals, or zooplankton, which in turn supply food for fish.

In the tidal zone and on shore, additional species of animals and plants are threatened. The problem in ports and harbors is compounded by the confined environment and the persistent levels of chronic pollution.

The influence of crude oil on the marine environment hinges on its fate in the ocean. Fresh from a tanker's hold or from an undersea well, the oil carries aromatic constituents that are toxic to marine life but which evaporate in a few days. Thus, oil in the English and Santa Barbara channels was less poisonous by the time it reached shore.

In addition to evaporation of aromatics and other volatile components, conversion processes change the composition of the crude oil. First, the oil and water mix, despite the old adage to the contrary. In fact, two types of emulsion are formed. The oil-in-water variety consists of droplets of oil which become stabilized by chemical action at their surfaces and then disperse across large areas.

The second emulsion, the water-in-oil type, is formed from droplets of water enclosed in sheaths of oil and is stabilized by various resinous and asphaltic materials natural in crude oil. The result is a floating, sticky, viscous mass that reminded someone of the dessert chocolate mousse and was nicknamed accordingly. This type of emulsion contains so much water that the bulk of emulsified material may exceed the original mass of oil.

Oil that survives the emulsive process is degraded by spontaneous oxidation and oxidation by microorganisms, the latter being the most powerful force of decomposition at sea.

Finally, if the oil is in the water for three months or more, a persistent asphaltic residue is left that may represent 15 per cent of the original volume. A similar residue collects on the sides and bottoms of the storage tanks of tankers or in the fuel tanks of oil-burning ships. Discharge of that waste accounts most often for the tar lumps that await bathers on many beaches of the world or that foul the nets of fishing boats and research vessels like that from the Woods Hole Oceanographic Institution.

Deterioration of crude oil reduces the immediate biological danger at sea, except to waterfowl. Cruises into oil-covered waters off Cornwall and California in general showed little initial damage to the critical layer of life just beneath the surface. . . .

Although a number of commercial fishermen in Santa Barbara disagree violently, U.S. and British scientists report that the oil did not affect the quantity or quality of fish. Echo soundings from the California research ship *Alaska* over a total of ninety-six miles in the polluted area revealed large schools of anchovy and eleven schools of unidentified fish. Midwater trawling brought in anchovies, California pompano, queenfish, jack mackerel, bonito, and other species. None seemed to be affected by the oil. Bottom trawling done in a later survey brought in a total of fifty-two different species which all appeared healthy.

Dredge samples from the bottom showed no oil contamination nor damage to fish and invertebrates. Samples from Santa Barbara Harbor, however, contained oil or oil emulsion, an indication of the danger in confined waters.

Possible damage to mammals that abound in the waters off California is a matter of conjecture that has not been resolved. For example, four dead porpoises, several seals, and six whales washed ashore after the oil leak began. The animals were coated with crude oil, but subsequent examinations have not linked the deaths to oil contamination. Results of examination of tissue from some of the whale carcasses by Federal investigators had not been made available by mid-June [1969]. However, in view of the fact that five California gray whales died from stranding in 1961, and three in 1964, the number did not seem unusually high to officials of the Los Angeles County Museum of Natural History.

According to provisional data gathered by the Nature Conservancy and the Royal Society for the Protection of Birds, more than 25,000 birds, mostly guillemots and razorbills, were killed by crude oil and chemical dispersants after the Torrey Canyon disaster. Puffins suffered heavily and the breeding populations of herring gulls and cormorants appeared to be reduced. The guillemot casualties equaled the entire breeding stock between the Isle of Wight and Cardigan Bay. Razorbill deaths equaled a third of the corresponding breeding stock. Of 7,849 birds brought to cleaning stations, only 450 were alive two months after the grounding.

The story was the same in California, only on a smaller scale. As of April 1, bird losses attributed to the oil totaled 3,500, according to the State Department of Fish and Game. As the leak continued, the toll pushed upward. The birds affected were mostly diving birds, such as grebes, cormorants, mergansers, pelicans, and loons. A total of 1,653 birds had been taken into cleaning stations, but only 198 had survived as of April 1 [1969], according to the State Department of Fish and Game.

Large amounts of oil were trapped in kelp beds off the California coast, Anacapa Island, and Santa Cruz Island. As with other organisms, mucous layers on the soft tissues apparently were a barrier to the oil, and even colonies of small bryozoan animals on the kelp were feeding normally. Similar findings were made in England.

Since weathered crude oil has lost much toxicity, the immediate threat ashore is from a smothering coat that cuts off air and light. In England, damage was limited to minor tainting of shellfish in the intertidal zone, the area bound by high-water and low-water extremes.

Surveys of marine populations on the rocks along the Cornish coasts revealed little damage. Even though completely covered by oil, 90 per cent of barnacles had managed to clear openings for themselves, according to Dr. J. Eric Smith, Director of the Plymouth Laboratory, Devon, England. Browsing limpets actually were about as effective in cleaning oil from the rocks as were chemical dispersants. Oil ingested by the animals apparently was bound into feces (whether digested or undigested was not clear), thus enhancing bacterial oxidation. The same phenomenon was noted in shore studies in California.

The California surveys showed more clearly the intertidal damage caused by crude oil. At East Cabrillo Beach, slicks were on the incoming tides during inspections in March and May following the blowout on January 28, reports Dr. Dale Straughan of the University of Southern California, Los Angeles. Dr. Straughan is project director of a study financed by a $220,000 grant from the Western Oil and Gas Association. Marine life in the upper intertidal zone was "virtually eliminated" by the slick, and oil layers on rocks prevented recolonization. Inspections at two other beaches showed that the usually numerous periwinkles had been displaced by oil, but that recolonization was possible. Examination of selected species, including certain mussels, acorn barnacles, and limpets, showed generally normal breeding activities except where the oil cover was heavy, an indication that animal life was recovering from the initial destruction.

Localized damage that may have been associated with the oil pollution also was reported by Dr. Wheeler J. North of the California Institute of Technology. He discovered that 10 to 15 per cent of the barnacle population had died on the underwater structure of Platform A where the blowout occurred and where the crude oil was fresh and still very toxic. In the heavily polluted Santa Barbara Harbor, about 60 per cent of mussels examined had died, but much of the destruction may have been caused by steam-cleaning operations to clear oil from the rocks.

Influence on Plant Life

The effect on plant life along the shore is uncertain. Scientists who prepared the British government report on the Torrey Canyon disaster concluded that salt marshes and mudflats were little damaged. However, Dr. D. S. Ranwell of the Nature Conservancy, Wareham, Dorset, reported that intertidal algae and lichens were killed on some rocky shorelines by smothering coats ol oil. On the Brittany coast, *Puccinellia maritima*, one of the chief types of grass in European salt marshes, and several other varieties were killed by Torrey Canyon oil that had weathered at sea for at least seven days.

On the other side of the world, observers from the California Department of Fish and Game reported little damage except to certain algae at Punta Arena, Santa Cruz Island, and to surfgrass on Anacapa Island that apparently was killed by the oil. . . .

Long-Term Effects

The cumulative effect of chronic as opposed to single massive oil spills has not been determined, but scientists suggest a number of discomforting possibilities. One derives from the research of Dr. R. J. Goldacre of Chester Beatty Research Institute, Fulham Road, London. He has shown that the membrane and granular contents of amoebae are irreversibly damaged and that the one-cell organisms die after long exposure to various fractions of crude oil. Repeated exposure to otherwise nonlethal doses of crude oil might have the same effect on single-cell planktonic organisms.

Furthermore, although the saturated hydrocarbon fractions with low boiling points have long been considered nontoxic, recent studies indicate that the low-boiling-point saturates are toxic to many lower forms of marine life, reported Dr. Max Blumer at the MIT meeting. Low concentrations can lead to anesthesia, higher concentrations to cellular destruction. In addition to the recognized toxicity from crude oil aromatics with low boiling points, such as benzene and toluene, the potential for cancer-inducing effects exists in the aromatics with higher boiling points. Such effects could be serious if introduced into the marine food chain, Dr. Blumer observed.

In the long run, the sheer volume of oil released at sea poses grave questions about ecological consequences. Loss of crude oil in oceans and in ports from accidents and intentional dumping amounts to 0.1 per cent of the total volume of oil transported at sea, Dr. Blumer estimated. He calculated that this totaled, conservatively, one million metric tons of crude oil spilled into the sea each year by man.

Dr. Blumer asserted that under these circumstances, human beings annually put into the ocean about as large a volume of hydrocarbons as do plants and animals. This is based on the calculation that the total biological productivity of the ocean equals about 30 billion metric tons of organic matter per year. About .01 per cent consists of natural hydrocarbons contained in the cells of plants and animals. This amounts to an input of approximately three million metric tons of natural hydrocarbons annually. If one matches against this total the estimate of at least one million tons of crude oil from shipping and port operations, oil from other shore activities, and oil from offshore wells, the amount put into the sea by man and by marine life are about equivalent, Dr. Blumer concluded. In addition, the production of natural hydrocarbons is fairly well dispersed throughout the oceans, he pointed out. Oil from human activities, on the other hand, is concentrated in shipping lanes and ports which often are in areas rich with marine life. . . .

Threat from Fuel Oil

In contrast to the potential long-term threat of crude oil, the deadliest effect of fuel oil is immediate toxicity, as in the following episodes:

On March 29, 1957, the Tampico Maru struck a rocky promontory in the Pacific 110 miles southeast of the U.S.-Mexican border; about one third of the cargo of 59,000 barrels of diesel fuel oil gushed into the sea. A month after the accident, oil slicks were still at sea and in tide pools, and action of the surf created a deadly sand-oil sludge in basins in the sea floor. Dead animals were found wherever beached debris had accumulated, reported consultants to Western Oil and Gas Association and investigator Wheeler J. North, California Institute of Technology. The odor of rotting animal tissue was detectable more than one hundred feet from the beach. The species most frequently affected were abalone, lobster, pismo clams, mussels, urchins, and sea stars. At shallow depths near the wreck, piles of dead sea urchins and mussels accumulated in sludge formed in the basins.

The 1968 breakup of the tanker Witwater on December 13, 1968, released diesel oil and "Bunker C" oil in the coral reefs and mangrove swamps at Galeta Island on the Caribbean Coast of the Canal Zone. Personnel at nearby Galeta Island Marine Station of the Smithsonian Tropical Research Institute began intensive scientific study of the biological effects of the pollution and instituted a long-term study. Initial reports from dives at Galeta Island showed: 50 per cent decrease in the number of tube worms, 90 per cent decrease in the number of certain starfish, 50 per cent decrease in the number of sponges, and 20 per cent decrease in the number of bristle worms. . . .

Competing Interests

Oil pollution also causes economic and esthetic damage. The economic interests of fishermen, for example, are substantial. Commercial fishermen in the United States caught

$454 million worth of fish and shellfish in 1966. Fresh and saltwater sport fishermen spend about $3 billion annually on their hobby; waterfowl hunters about $85 million.

Representative cases in which oil tainting made shellfish unedible were described by Dr. A. C. Simpson of the Fisheries Laboratory, Burnham-on-Crouch, England . . .

1. An oil spill in Poole harbor, England, in 1961 halted the sale of edible winkles, a type of snail, in a number of areas for several months. The shells were stained with oil that tainted entire batches during cooking.

2. Partially emulsified oil in Morecambe Bay some years ago produced small globules that were taken by mussels, cockles, and oysters. The flesh was tainted and mussel fishing was suspended for about two weeks.

3. The persistent, low-level oil pollution that bedevils many coastal areas is exemplified by the situation in South-ampton Water, where clams often acquire an oil flavor that can be dissipated only by relocating them in clean water.

Besieged public-relations officials of oil companies and distraught officials of seaside communities in the United States, England, the European continent, and elsewhere have tried to counteract the bleak effects of oil-clogged beaches with soothing words, but residents, tourists, and vacationers have not been comforted. The acrid stench of crude oil could be detected for five miles at sea in the Torrey Canyon disaster and at times up to two miles inland in the Santa Barbara incident. Dark-brown crude oil washing in actually smoth-ered the surf in many areas, an obviously distressing sight to ocean bathers.

Union Oil personnel labored to clean the beaches in California, but their determined work often was undone the next day by fresh oil. Beaches elsewhere were cleaned by man or the action of the waves only to be inundated days or weeks later by oil released from kelp beds. Oil treated with dispersants on Cornish beaches sunk into the sands, to be exposed months later by wind and sea. Thick mats of crude oil on some beaches in France formed huge black masses that were too expensive to remove.

In addition to esthetic values, recreation interests have a great deal at stake. For example, a major oil-pollution incident off Long Island during summer months might cost as much as $30 million in lost tourist business, according to estimates in the special report on oil pollution to former President Johnson. If Platform A had been located off the Los Angeles area beaches instead of eighty miles northwest, the amount could have totaled $51 million.

Countermeasures Unreliable

The difficulties caused by oil pollution are magnified by lack of adequate technical countermeasures. The method employed most extensively off the California coast was to scatter straw into the oil, then collect the oil-laden material as it washed on shore. The system was laborious but effective and was similar to the approach used successfully off France after the Torrey Canyon grounding.

Another approach, fighting chemicals with chemicals, has proven extremely dangerous on a large scale, since the dispersants are potentially far more toxic than the oil they disperse. Another drawback is the expense. The chemicals used at sea and on shore after the Torrey Canyon disaster, cost more than $1.5 million. The cost did not include the expense of application.

A number of mechanical devices were employed or suggested for use off California and England. These included various booms with below-water skirts or air-jet attachments as physical barriers to contain the oil for later collection by suction, rotating drum, or large sleeve-like containers. The methods were effective, but impractical in heavy seas and too slow in face of the gigantic amounts of oil.

Precision bombing of the Torrey Canyon wreck burned about 20,000 tons of oil. The technique was, of course, dangerous and not applicable against large oil slicks already at sea. Chemicals have been developed to support controlled burning of oil at sea, but they are expensive and unproven. In addition, one can imagine the consternation of the residents of Santa Barbara if the oil in the channel were periodically burned to produce a pall of acrid black smoke that simply converted water pollution to air pollution. Furthermore, the residue after burning is a black mass that is easier to collect than raw crude oil but which still requires a gigantic clean-up effort with as yet undesigned equipment.

About twenty types of high-density granular materials have been suggested for sinking oil at sea. In the Bay of Biscay off the coast of France, about 3,000 tons of powdered chalk with sodium stearate added was used to sink a mass of oil that totaled about 20,000 tons. One drawback is that oil sunk in this fashion may endanger fishing grounds, particularly in shallow water. The long-term consequences of the mass sunk in the Bay of Biscay are undeterminable.

The British government report on the Torrey Canyon urges improved methods to increase the possibility of recovering the oil from a stranded tanker by pumping it off. Consideration also was given to immobilizing the oil in the Torrey Canyon by jelling, freezing with solid carbon dioxide, or mechanical means, but these methods were rejected as impractical.

Pessimistic Outlook

In view of the worldwide contamination from oil and the lack of reliable countermeasures, scientists who surveyed the general havoc and disruption caused by the wreck of the Torrey Canyon were not hopeful about the future. Concluded the authors of the detailed report on the Torrey Canyon by the Plymouth Laboratory entitled *Torrey Canyon: Pollution and Marine Life:* "We are progressively making a slum of nature and may eventually find that we are enjoying the benefit of science and industry under conditions which no civilized society should tolerate."

TOWARD A WATER POLLUTION POLICY [5]

All of us are striving for a better understanding of what can and should be done in the future by industry and government in the field of water pollution abatement. . . . None of us would want to suggest that industry—or indeed, any other segment of society—has the special wisdom to set forth an appropriate national policy and make it work. But by the same token, industry can contribute to the development of sound policy, and has a continuing role to play in its execution.

In this context, there are four points I want to discuss: the way we approach the problem; the costs; the criteria we set up; the basic role that the public must play in deciding what the goals will be. . . .

First, the way we approach the problem. If an effective national policy is to be created, it must be based on the pollution problem as a whole, and not just its separate parts. In some of our past actions, we have honored this principle in the breach. Rather than point the finger at anyone else, let me give you an example from my own company.

At one of our plants, several years ago, it became necessary to remove more solids from plant wastes, in order to meet new standards that were to be adopted by a local regulatory agency. A filtration system was installed. The system solved the water problem, but the inorganic solids then had to be disposed of in a landfill, and the organic solids had to be burned. The landfill caused no difficulty. However, the incinerator wasn't efficient enough to handle the organic solids, so there was an air pollution problem. Installing a more efficient incinerator took care of that, but the incinerator made so much noise we began to get complaints from the neighbors. Finally, we installed an elaborate muffling system that cut down the noise, and only

[5] From "Toward a Policy on Pollution," remarks by Charles B. McCoy, president, E. I. du Pont de Nemours & Company, to Executives' Conference on Water Pollution Abatement, United States Department of the Interior, Washington, D.C., October 24, 1969. The Author. E. I. du Pont de Nemours & Company, Inc. Wilmington, Del. 19898.

then was the problem really solved. Perhaps this type of example has a familiar ring to some of you.

Industry is not alone in the piecemeal attack on pollution. In government, too, there have been separate efforts to solve separate parts of the problem. In some degree this may have been inevitable, for the scale of the problem has made it necessary for the government to divide it into manageable pieces. However, in the process of subdividing direction and control, we have not always had adequate coordination among agencies and programs. At times different agencies have given us overlapping or conflicting guidelines to follow. Occasionally, one level of government or one agency has set forth standards at variance with the standards of another agency, in an area where both have jurisdiction. Until the confusion has been straightened out, progress has been held up.

I don't intend this as criticism of any particular agency. To the contrary, the point is raised only to stress the fact that many of us have been approaching interrelated problems in bits and pieces. We have worked on water pollution or air pollution or solid waste problems or noise problems— as though each existed independently.

All the time we've been doing this, ecologists have been trying to tell us that the environment is a closed system; that everything in it—including man—is interdependent. We accept that idea in principle, but don't always carry it over to the day-to-day fight against pollution. . . .

The Cost/Benefit Equation

As a second element in our thinking, we must pay more attention to the cost-benefit equation. . . . It is very clear to me that most of the steps we take together to solve our pollution problems are going to have to be measured by an economic yardstick. Industry cannot afford, nor can the nation afford, to do the maximum job of pollution abatement everywhere or all at once. We would all like to be more optimistic about this. Everybody would be delighted if Du Pont or some other company could report that it has found a way to turn the expense of pollution control into an asset. It just isn't possible.

To be sure, the chemical industry has been trying to find ways to retrieve useful materials from liquid outfalls and stack gases. A few of these efforts have succeeded. But most have failed because of the economics involved. We'll keep on trying, but as we look to the future we must be realistic. Most of the economically valuable products that might be recovered from effluents already are being recovered. From now on, with a few exceptions, what goes down the pipe or up the stack has to be considered as waste with little or no value. The question is what to do with it, and that question is proving to be expensive to answer.

Du Pont's total investment in pollution control facilities now totals more than $125 million. We spend about $26 million a year to operate and maintain these facilities. The equivalent of nearly 1,000 full-time employees are engaged in pollution control work and antipollution research. Like most companies today, Du Pont considers this to be an integral part of the cost of doing business. All of us should be entirely candid about this, not only with each other but with the public as well. Any significant improvement on a national scale is going to cost major amounts of money and affect the prices people pay for products, or show up in their tax bill.

This leads to a third observation: We can help keep the costs within reason by setting goals that permit different standards in different areas. In water pollution, for example, legislation must apply equitably to all jurisdictions, but if the guidelines are made identical for every river or lake system, the overall costs will be astronomical.

In our view the best approach is to base laws and regulations on the uses people have in mind for different lakes and rivers, and on the specific characteristics of each water system.

As we all know, different streams have different properties
—width, depth, flow rate. They differ in their ability to
purify themselves. Some are in densely populated areas where
the water is used primarily as an artery of transportation.
Others are in resort and recreation areas we want to protect
for swimming. To put all these under a single set of standards would be prohibitively expensive. To establish arbitrary percentage guidelines would be even worse.

Above all, we must avoid simplistic formulas. If, for instance, we require each industrial company to reduce what
it is putting into a river by some fixed percentage, we would
be attaching a special penalty to the companies that have
made the biggest efforts to reduce pollution. They may have
already cut down on their effluents by process changes and
in-plant controls. To ask them to reduce the residual by 75
or 85 per cent would put them in a severe cost bind, and
be grossly unjust.

Other companies that have done less and spent less
would be favored. They would start at a higher base point,
and could meet the percentage requirement more easily.
Thus, the percentage approach would have exactly the op-
posite effect from what is wanted. It would help the foot-
draggers and hurt the leaders.

We must make improvements in the quality of our rivers
and streams—that is agreed—but we want to buy the right
amount of improvement for the right kind of money. Criteria
based on intended use, acknowledging the different characteristics of different bodies of water, and giving credit for
improvements already made, would help us meet that goal.

What Criteria for Antipollution Measures?

That brings up an obvious question. What is the right
amount of improvement, and who says so? Here, the cost-
benefit equation moves beyond the realm of dollars alone.

In part, the question has technical overtones, with special
reference to the chemical industry. We can help identify improvements that can be handled with existing technology.

We can point out some areas where present technology has not been fully utilized, and where better application would save all of us money. We can come up with cost estimates on various alternatives, and offer some judgments about the types of R&D [Research and Development] projects that look most promising and timely.

We have only scratched the surface in R&D. To offer a few examples, I'm told that very little is known about the effects on living organisms of low-level exposure to pollutants over long periods of time. We have only begun to explore the relationships of various contaminants to our ecology. We are still far away from an adequate mathematical description of natural water systems subject to pollution. We lack knowledge about the molecular nature of substances in these water systems.

But we have made a start, and we have a good idea of what to do next. . . . [In September 1969] a subcommittee of the American Chemical Society released a major report on the environment. This is much more than just another study. It is a technically sound statement of what needs to be done, and it includes dozens of specific recommendations for research, development, and engineering projects. A number of these fall within our competence in the chemical industry, and some are projects on which work is already under way.

R&D is only part of the answer. There are still questions of cost and priority, and these are questions that only the public can answer. How much is the nation willing to pay? How much environmental improvement can we undertake without jeopardizing the nation's economic health? How much of our R&D should be focused here? Must we defer action on other national problems which may be just as pressing?

These are not business or technical questions. They are public and social judgments. The answers can come only from the people. Thus, to state the fourth point, it seems to me that the Federal Government has a primary and basic role to play in measuring the public's wishes, and shaping an appropriate national policy.

No other organization in society has a charter to speak for the nation as a whole. The Federal Government is the only organization that can draw together the many views that have to be accommodated. The states and municipalities, and certainly private industry, must look to the Federal level not just for coordination and specific legislation, but first of all for a clear, consistent statement of the national will. . . .

Industry's role, as I see it, is one of active involvement in all aspects of this work. A great many corporations have had years of experience in pollution control, and these companies represent a rich source of practical knowledge as well as research capability. We can apply more of this practical knowledge without waiting for all of the results to come in from research. In Du Pont, we have been trying to make contributions in a number of areas.

In terms of our own manufacturing operations, we adopted a firm policy many years ago: No new plant may be built, no new process approved, unless the plans include workable methods of waste disposal or treatment. The methods must meet or exceed all legal requirements. We are trying to bring our older plants and processes into line with the same policy.

On our staff, working in pollution control, are technologists in many fields, including chemistry, engineering, toxicology, medicine, meteorology, and the biological sciences. Many of these experts are active in assisting and advising organizations outside the company. These include various industry associations and civic and governmental groups concerned with pollution abatement.

Du Pont has developed equipment to detect, measure, and analyze various pollutants and to help reduce or modify emissions. These include an instrument for monitoring stack emissions; a catalyst support used in fume abatement; fibers especially suited for use in dust-collecting filter bags; liners of synthetic rubber for brine pits in oil fields; a manifold reactor which greatly reduces hydrocarbon emissions from automobiles; and a reverse osmosis device which has a number of applications, such as desalting brackish water and helping to purify industrial waste streams.

Other companies have also developed devices, products, and technical information which can be of great value in our common fight against pollution.

All of these are available to help in the national effort. Perhaps if we work more closely with one another, on a cooperative basis, we can find more ways to pull these contributions together and make them more effective.

IV. A LAND TO LIVE IN

EDITOR'S INTRODUCTION

For many decades we thought of conservation mainly in terms of our great natural heritage, our wilderness lands and more especially our national parks. In this section the present plight of what we think of as these protected areas is considered. But today, if we think of "America the beautiful" ("America the [formerly] beautiful" as one author quoted below suggests), we move to the landscape of our urban areas and farmlands to find that our population pressures alone are blighting the land with great ugliness, trash, and overuse.

First, the wilderness lands and one of our national parks —the Everglades—are dealt with in articles appearing in *Life* and *Look*. Then, James Nathan Miller in a *Reader's Digest* report surveys the results of our mounting population in terms of the beauty and resources of our land. A discussion of the problem of our refuse, our trash, by Edwin A. Roberts, Jr. of *The National Observer* follows. And, finally, Neal Stanford, a staff correspondent of *The Christian Science Monitor*, explains a project that looks hopefully toward a time in the future when all wastes of our technological society can be eliminated without creating new problems in terms of trash or new pollutants in our countryside or waterways.

AMERICA'S ENDANGERED LANDSCAPE [1]

The wilderness . . . lands—10 million acres now under protection, almost all west of the Mississippi—have always held

[1] From editorial. *Life*. 67:32. Ag. 1, '69. *Life* Magazine Editorial, August 1, 1969, © 1969 Time Inc. Reprinted by permission.

a magic. F. Scott Fitzgerald wrote of the early settlers arriving
at the new world three centuries ago:

> For a transitory enchanted moment man must have held his
> breath in the presence of this continent, compelled into an esthetic
> contemplation he neither understood nor desired, face to face for
> the last time in history with something commensurate to his capac-
> ity for wonder.

That enchanted moment is long past. The continental
wilderness has largely vanished, and what remains of it is
threatened by our own increasing needs. Our capacity for
wonder survives, but less survives to be wondered at.

Vanishing wilderness is, however, only one aspect of the
deteriorating quality of American life today, both in the
countryside and in our cities. There are many others: pollution, endangered wildlife, smog, urban sprawl and that new
catch-all term *uglification*. . . .

Change, of course, is inevitable; and progress, which is
intelligently conceived change, is desirable. There must indeed be more jet airports, highways, housing and power
plants, and it is foolish to maintain—as some conservationists do—that their encroachment must be prevented everywhere and at all costs. But too often the cost is too high. We
are a rich country, but as Jean Mayer, a population expert
and Special Consultant to the President, writes in *Columbia
Forum:* "Rich people occupy much more space, consume
more of each natural resource, disturb the ecology more, and
create more land, air, water, chemical, thermal and radioactive pollution than poor people."

The population of the United States is headed toward 300
million in the next quarter of a century; our GNP [gross
national product] will reach a trillion dollars in the next two
years. This explosive combination of people and money will
produce ever greater demands for more cars, dams, lumber,
fuel, food, roads, land. These demands will lead, unless
checked, to more pollution, garbage, trash, noise, desecration
—and leave much less beauty to evoke our capacity for
wonder.

What we now require is an intelligent and continuing weighing of the demands of "progress" against what might be sacrificed to them. Fortunately, some momentum in this direction already exists. Both government and industry have shown awareness—though not yet enough—of the environmental side effects of their activities. The Wilderness Act of 1964 set aside vital acreage for protection and provides a method for setting aside much more. Two months ago [May 1969] President Nixon established an Environmental Quality Council at Cabinet level, with himself as chairman and his scientific adviser Dr. Lee DuBridge as executive secretary. The same executive order set up a Citizens' Advisory Committee on Environmental Quality, with Laurance Rockefeller as its chairman. Both groups have a broad charter but have yet to show what they can do. Such industries as chemicals, oil and utilities have recently shown a greater responsibility toward the environment in which they flourish.

Public concern has also increased. The destruction of rivers by chemicals and detergents, the destruction of wildlife by insecticides, the destruction of landscape by indiscriminate and ruthless "development"—all are now less likely to occur without protest than was possible ten years ago.

Nevertheless, not nearly enough information exists to enable government, industry and the public to determine whether or not specific projects should be approved. The Santa Barbara oil-drilling leases, granted by the United States Department of the Interior, might not have been granted if the full extent of the threat had been known. The use of DDT, a successful chemical against insects, is either being questioned or has been banned in seventeen states because its damage to other forms of life is finally recognized. Marshlands that have been filled in and gobbled up by industry and housing might well have been protected if more people had realized that one acre of marshland potentially can produce ten times as much animal protein (fish, oysters, clams, crabs) as one acre of farmland.

Quite aside from the purely physical destruction involved in careless exploitation are the esthetic losses. Even when no ecological damage is committed, we constantly afflict the eye with shoddy excrescences of bad design, ugly and haphazard travesties of modernity spattered across the landscape in the name of expansion.

OUR THREATENED WILDERNESS LANDS [2]

The wilderness erodes. What remains of it survives in isolated and glorious patches, on mountainsides and remote islands and dark swamps and deserts. For every strip that's left there are competing claims, often more than two; the back country may be serene, but there is little security. . . . Hells Canyon, the continent's deepest gorge, threatened with inundation by a reservoir; Yosemite, already inundated with people; Corkscrew Swamp, a teeming pool of life endangered by water-draining canals; the Pine Barrens of New Jersey, a tidy forest being eyed by the jetport builders; Admiralty Island, Alaska, domain of grizzlies and bald eagles, headed for the power saws of the loggers. "Something will have gone out of us as a people," Wallace Stegner has written, "if we ever let the remaining wilderness be destroyed." The wilderness erodes. And as it does, perhaps we do too. . . .

Our history was written in prairies and mountains, not castles and cathedrals, and the raw spectacle confronted by the first Europeans on this shore had no equal in the Old World. Americans still live so close to the wilderness, figuratively if not often in fact, that it's difficult for many to see that it is practically gone. It doesn't *look* that way, flying over the country at 28,000 feet, but almost all that land down there is spoken for—it's being used to graze cattle or sheep, it's part of a military base or a testing site, it's been leased to a lumber company. Excluding Alaska, only between 2 and 3 per cent of the United States qualifies for the Federal definition of wilderness: "An area where the earth and its com-

² From "Threatened America," by Donald Jackson, staff writer. *Life.* 67:33-43. Ag. 1, '69. © 1969 Time Inc. Reprinted by permission.

munity of life are untrammeled by man, where man himself
is a visitor who does not remain . . . [an area] without permanent improvement or human habitation."

Most of that slender remnant has either been picked over
once, or is about to be. The Wilderness Act of 1964 set aside
9 million acres for permanent preservation (a million more
acres have been added since then), but left the remaining
de facto wilderness as a shrinking arena where the final
scenes of an old American drama are being played—the conflict between the developers and the conservationists.

In the past the fight has never been even. From the beginning, when the last Conestoga was put on blocks and the
boosters fanned into the countryside, building the dam has
had clear precedence over listening to the river, clearing the
woods has had the edge on getting lost in them. There have
been isolated victories for the conservationists through the
years—it comes as a revelation to learn that Yellowstone Park
was set aside as a "public park or pleasuring ground" *ninety-
seven years ago*—but those were exceptions.

The American creed was and is foursquare for growth;
growth is seen to have a sort of *a priori* goodness, a moral
value, and against that force the tender arguments of the
wilderness-lovers ("deep breathers" and "kissers of the wind,"
one developer calls them) were feeble indeed. Still, there was
an ambivalence in the American mind: if conquest of the
wilderness seemed necessary and therefore Christian and
laudable, it was gradually subverted by the idea of wilderness
as sanctuary, as escape, as the resting place of truth and
beauty. It's a tough one: both ideas are wholly American,
both impulses beat in the American breast, and thus the conflict is not so much a clash of two opposing groups as it is a
collision of two ideas within the mind of each of us. "We
have met the enemy," Pogo said, "and they are us."

Saving Hells Canyon

Both sides indulge in what might be called the "last
great" syndrome. In Hells Canyon on the Idaho-Oregon

border, for example, private and public power companies
have hankered to build a dam for half a generation, claiming that the middle Snake River represents the "last great
source of hydroelectric power in the Pacific Northwest." The
Sierra Club, a late-arriving but fiercely effective foe of any
dam in the canyon, ripostes with the charge that the Snake
is the "last great free-flowing river in the West." Both con-
tentions are wrong, and both sides, in moments when candor
gets the better of combat, will admit it.

But now the fight is a lot closer to even than it ever was.
The reason, probably the only reason that could explain it,
is that the public, or at least large segments of it measurable
regularly in election returns, has become conservation-
minded.

Nothing like reliable statistics are available to document
this phenomenon, but its existence is conceded by both dam
builders and river preservers, the former with a sour mutter
that "the pendulum has swung too far the other way," and
the latter with the kind of raucous victory shout peculiar to
long-time losers.

Nirvana for the deep breathers is still beyond the sunset,
however. David Brower, the eloquent conservationist recently ousted from leadership of the Sierra Club, explains that
"there's plenty of power when the public gets excited about
a specific issue like Grand Canyon or the redwoods, but
there's still not enough day-in day-out support."

Brower's examples are not random; preservation of the
Grand Canyon (from a dam which would have backed reservoir water into the canyon) and the redwoods (from the
lumber industry) were victories for an army he commanded.
Through dogged energy and charismatic flair, Brower built
the Sierra Club to its present strength and letter-writing
clout. In April [1969] he was voted out of office. Critics
charged that he was authoritarian, spent too freely and
acted without the consent of the club's board of directors. As
a result, the conservationists are floundering momentarily
for lack of strong leadership. The two most significant and

visible leaders of the last decade, Brower and former Interior Secretary Stewart Udall, are currently without portfolio.

The best illustration of the growing strength of the wilderness forces is the sunburst of conservation legislation that emerged from Congress during the Johnson years. The Wilderness Act was only one of dozens that reflected an increasing environmental uneasiness—the scenic rivers bill, antipollution laws, establishment of new parks and others.

In the courts as well, the values of wilderness have begun to get a hearing. A Federal appeals court ruled in 1965 that scenic, historic and recreational values had to be taken into account by the Consolidated Edison Company in its proposal to build a nuclear power plant on the Hudson River. A 1967 United States Supreme Court decision on the Hells Canyon dam issue introduced the same ideas into an order remanding the question to the Federal Power Commission, where it remains.

Industry and Conservation

Industry itself has begun to show some long-absent sensitivity to conservation. Public relations men go to elaborate lengths to avoid offending the wind-kissers. Some firms have subsidized conservation studies, others have donated parks or wild land to local governments. This kind of thing cuts no ice with Brower, however. He calls it "cosmetics for rape." He is, of course, incorrigible.

Along with the growing power of the conservationists has come a change in the character of the movement. The wind-kissers, in fact, are in decline. The scientists, more specifically the ecologists, are increasingly important. Nowadays a stand of trees or a piece of sageland is worth preserving not necessarily for its beauty or its opportunity for solitude; it is more likely defended as vital to the balance of nature, the "chain of life" in a given area, or as a natural laboratory containing potentially valuable secrets. The ecologists talk less about the romance of wilderness and more about eco-

systems, distinctive networks of relationships between land
and water, vegetation and wildlife.

This has led to some peculiar gyrations. Some scientists
are trying to quantify, in the good new American way, the
values of wilderness. This is a ploy born in desperation. For
decades developers have been able to show, in dreary charts
of "cost-benefit ratios," what *specifically* might be gained
from whatever project they have in mind—read: dollars. In
reply the conservationists have fiddled with their fingernails
and talked about beauty. Now they are groping for figures
to fight the developers on their own terms; hence graphs that
measure "scale of valley character" and assign numerical
values to a view of a mountain or the presence of a bear.

"What it comes down to is this," says Brower. "If you
can't measure a thing, measure it anyway for those who won't
know anything about it unless you do."

The ecologists are running the palace, all right, but the
troubadours are still skulking around outside in the high
grass, practicing birdsongs, comparing backpacks, listening,
frowning when they hear an airplane. Udall thinks the two
sides, conservationists and developers, now have "a kind of
parity of influence," but most conservationists disagree.
"There's very little conservation legislation coming forward
these days," says one congressman. "The logging and power
interests are still damned strong. I'm pessimistic."

The one huge, dark fact dominating the entire question
of land preservation is continued population growth. Any
question of conserving space leads ultimately to a question
of limiting the people with claims on that space. Most defenders of the wilderness are, at bottom, pessimistic about
their chances, and spiraling population is the reason. It
seems the final, ironic fruition of the "more is better" phi-
losophy—to simply outgrow our resources. Nothing riles
conservationists more than the celebration of growth for its
own sake—ceremonies saluting the arrival of the 200 mil-
lionth American, the National Park Service's breathless re-

leases on rising attendance figures. A Sierra Club poster is only about 20 per cent facetious when it suggests that man, like the bald eagle or the flamingo, is now an endangered species.

Another dark shadow on the future of wilderness is the state of public ignorance. Despite the growth of interest in the outdoors, most Americans remain urban, motorized and oblivious to the physical and spiritual wonders of the wild. The major recreation phenomenon of the past few years is the growth of trailers and camper trucks, motel rooms on wheels with names like Teardrop, Week-N-Der, Six-Pac, Rolls-Royal and CharAkee. Most camper drivers get no closer to the wild than a national park campground.

On the other hand, though most Americans may personally feel no urge to tramp the back country, they are enchanted by the idea of its existence. The camper truck may become an outdoors teaser: as he sees a little of raw, splendid America, the driver may want to see more; he may even recognize that the easiest way is not necessarily the best way —but that's getting giddy.

For the men who draw up master plans and long-range policy, then, there is this difficult series of questions: what does the majority want, open country or scenic overlooks? Do you strike a balance between tourist development and wilderness preservation and, if so, how? Is *everything* that remains worth saving, or just some of it? (When conservation pioneer Bob Marshall was asked how much wilderness was enough, he replied, "How many Brahms symphonies are enough?" He was incorrigible too.) How do we develop an ecological conscience in America? Through education, but why haven't we done so? Why aren't children taught to respect all living things? Wilderness is peculiar among American possessions in that it is not susceptible to compromise. To take some wilderness is still to take wilderness. Roads cannot be unbuilt.

What Conservationists Want

The men who worry about these questions have come up with a few suggestions. (No ideas or initiatives have come from the new Administration, except for the President's creation of an Environmental Quality Council. "We're trying to steer clear of the controversial ones right at the start," says a high Interior Department official.) Here are the proposals:

1. The National Park Service is considering eliminating cars from some parks and operating campgrounds on a reservation system, as opposed to the present first-come, first-served method.

2. Some conservationists have urged that tax relief be granted to encourage the preservation of open space. Pay landowners, in effect, not to develop their land.

3. Udall suggests that "environmental mediators" could arbitrate disputes between developers and conservationists, in the manner of labor mediators.

4. Brower would like to see a sort of Fair Conservation Practices Commission, an independent nongovernmental agency with authority to review projects before and after construction.

5. Biologist Garrett Hardin proposes that access to wilderness be limited to those "of great physical vigor," willing and able to walk and to take the risks of the wild, and that wilderness and park areas be established at graded levels of difficulty according to ability.

Hardin's intriguing idea recognizes the final paradox: as more people learn to know and appreciate wilderness, more will want to experience it. Ultimately, their numbers might destroy it just as effectively as would highways or snack bars. It could be cherished to death.

[See "Establishment of Council of Environmental Advisers" in Section V, below for proposals for pollution control made by the Nixon Administration subsequent to publication of this article.—Ed.]

THE ASSAULT ON THE EVERGLADES [3]

Death dances with life in the Everglades, in the nature of things. Smallest life succumbs to larger forms, which are eaten in turn: an endless circle of innocent murder. Vegetation struggles for rootholds, lives, dies, rots, revives. To know the Everglades is to confront the intimate relatedness of living things; to know death as an accomplice to life.

Now death with a difference haunts the Everglades. Death by starvation: the natural flow of groundwater—the Park's life-bearing plasma—has been diverted to prosper rampant economic development. Death by poison: a big jetport complex, just begun, would pollute the Park's air and water. Under siege, the Everglades faces a final death.

The alligator is the king-link in the Everglades food chain, the eater who is not eaten. Once he is three years old and three feet long, he has no natural enemy. Except man, who used to send hatchling alligators through the mails as souvenirs of perverse nature love; and who still, illegally, rips the skin from the alligator's belly to make $300 handbags and $150 shoes, leaving the rest to rot. Even if he survives man's incursions into his habitat, for the sake of man's foppery the Everglades alligator faces extinction.

The roar of machines manicuring thirty-nine square miles of cypress is only an overture to the raucous symphony of big jets: 150,000 landings and takeoffs a year, at the start; 900,000—more than one a minute, day and night—at full tilt. One runway is ready to go, just seven miles from the Park. But conservationists have forced a belated review of any further development. Life in the Everglades has won a reprieve.

[3] From "The Assault on the Everglades," by Anthony Wolff, a senior editor. *Look*. 33:44-50+. S. 9, '69. By permission of the editors. From the September 9, 1969 issue of *Look* Magazine. Copyright 1969 by Cowles Communications, Inc. (On January 15, 1970, the Nixon Administration announced an agreement with the state and local authorities in Florida forbidding the construction of a major international jetport near the Everglades National Park. This agreement thus seems to avert the latest of the dangers to which the Everglades have been subjected.—Ed.)

The ultimate fate of the Everglades National Park may not be apparent for years, even decades, but it is being decided right now. Preservationists are wrestling with developers over crucial questions of water management and land development. If the preservationists win, the Park may survive in a near-natural state, while the virulent growth of south Florida will be controlled. If the developers prevail, the Park will eventually die. The fight for this unique wild land at the southeastern extremity of America is of more than incidental importance to a prodigal nation growing poor in wilderness.

On the preservationists' map, the whole interior of south Florida is a shallow basin, barely above sea level. Through this basin during the wet season flows a river fifty miles across and only inches deep, seeping south and west through saw grass, cypress and mangrove, all the way from Lake Okeechobee to Florida Bay and the Gulf of Mexico. In its meanderings, the water accumulates a rich suspension of minute plant and animal life, essential to life in the Everglades National Park.

The developers—chambers of commerce, land speculators, agri-businessmen and the like—plot their moves on a different map of the same south Florida. Their map resembles the New York City subway system more than anything in nature, with surveyor-straight canals radiating from Lake Okeechobee. By diverting the natural flow of groundwater, short-cutting it to the sea, the canals make land speculators into alchemists, able to transmute river bottom into dry land and dry land into pure gold.

The natural profusion of life, disorderly, varied, self-sufficient, gives way to endless rows of pampered citrus trees, converging toward the flat horizon in unnatural regimental formation, less like living things than plastic plants set out by an obsessed geometrician; or to endless rows of cookie-cutter houses, each offering its owner a piece of paradise. Obviously, the same surface water that is the Everglades' life-blood is nothing more than red ink to the developers, and the stage is set for the present conflict.

Florida's Development and the Everglades

Actually, the Everglades began to lose out on the question of water rights as far back as the 1880s, when an enterprising visionary named Hamilton Disston saw farmland where there was endless swamp, and built the first drainage canals from Lake Okeechobee to the sea.

Canal building on a massive scale did not begin until much later, until the population of south Florida had grown to the point where the lake's occasional floods meant great loss of human life and property, and drainage canals were authorized as flood-control devices. By 1948, the year after a million and a half acres of south Florida had been secured for preservation as a national park, the natural flow of water to the Everglades was put in the hands of the Central and Southern Florida Flood Control Project.

From the start, the project was promised by the United States Army Corps of Engineers as protection to "assist in restoring and maintaining natural conditions within the National Park." The National Park Service accepted this and similar language from the Corps of Engineers and others as adequate assurance that the Park would get from the Project the same flow of water it used to get from nature.

The test came in 1962, when a levee across the Park's northern boundary was completed during the worst drought in Florida history. In order to assure water for irrigation in the agricultural areas north of the Park, the flow of water to the Everglades was stopped. In 1963, as the drought continued, the Everglades National Park received not one drop of water from the Project's levees. In 1964, another dry year, the Park was granted less than 2 per cent of its minimum annual requirement.

The result was that the agricultural interests north of the Park survived the drought, while much of the life in the

Park did not. Millions of animals died as the water table sank lower and lower, exposing the bottoms of ponds and waterways to harden and crack in the Florida sun. The Park Service dug wells to give some relief and collected uncounted thousands of animal corpses. Animals that survived failed to breed normally, or turned cannibal and ate their own off-spring. In the estuarine fringes of the Park, salt water advanced inland, unimpeded by the pressure of fresh-water flow, altering the delicate chemistry of spawning grounds and rookeries.

The drought ended, and was followed by several seasons of abundant rainfall. Life revived in the Park, but only tentatively, as though its man-made agony had deprived life in the Everglades of its natural drive for abundance; as though life itself were anticipating the next dry spell, when man will again covet the Park's water.

Two things are certain for the future: there will be, sooner or later, another drought; and south Florida, glut-tonous for growth, ambitious for eminence among the meg-alopolises of the world, will make ever greater demands on the area's limited water resources. In view of these certain-ties, can the Everglades National Park survive?

Who Speaks for the Park?

Those who speak most forcefully for the Park's future—including the Sierra Club, the Audubon Society, the National Park Service, and many members of Congress—insist that there must be a formal agreement among the Park Service, the Flood Control District and the Corps of Engineers, establishing minimum water rights and schedules for the Park. According to their formula, the Park would share both water scarcity and water abundance with existing development in the area; but the Park would be protected against claims on its water supply by future development. In short, the Park would no longer be at the mercy of progress, south-Florida-style.

Neither the Corps of Engineers nor the Flood Control District has so far been willing to endorse such a formula. The Corps claims it lacks jurisdiction over the operation of the Project, on which it has already spent $170 million of the taxpayers' money, even though the Chief of Engineers' original plan included this power. Until a formal agreement is reached, the water table in the Everglades National Park will fluctuate according to the dictates of the Flood Control District authorities, whose interests may lie elsewhere.

Even while the question of the *quantity* of water for the Park remains unsettled, the *quality* of that water is threatened by the new Miami jetport, already under construction near the Park's northern border. The airport will eventually be five times as large as New York's Kennedy, with two six-mile runways to handle the biggest planes. The jetport's promoters confidently promise that a large city will grow up around the airport. Until now, none of the many agencies involved seems to have given adequate thought to the pollution that the airport and its surrounding development will release into water headed for the Park.

In fact, statements by responsible county and airline officials seem to appropriate the National Park wilderness as a "sound screen" and a "buffer" for airport thunder.

The initial runway, a federally financed pilot-training facility, is nearly completed. At this late date, the county has responded to pressure from supporters of the Park, at least to the extent of commissioning an independent study of the effects of the airport on the environment, and possible alternative sites. Whatever the results of that study, there is no assurance that the county will be willing to abandon years of ambitious planning, even if that is the only thing that will save the Park.

Last June [1969], the Senate Interior and Insular Affairs Committee, considering the plight of the Everglades, heard from Senator Gaylord Nelson [Democrat, Wisconsin]:

Either the Federal Aviation Agency doesn't give any more money for planning the airport, the Corps stops all its building, the

Department of Transportation doesn't provide aid for a highway in
there until all questions are settled, or else we publicly confess right
now that we have decided that we are going to go ahead and destroy
the Park. I don't think there is any other answer.

POPULATION AND THE LANDSCAPE [4]

Forty miles up the Hudson River from New York harbor
there is a magnificent gorge so striking in beauty and so rich
in history that many consider it one of the most precious
spots in America. Here the Hudson, reaching the end of its
wide avenue between the sloping apple orchards and dairy
farms of the old Dutch patroon country, gathers itself into a
channel between two 1,000-foot granite cliffs—Storm King
Mountain on its west side, Breakneck Ridge on its east. Only
an hour's drive from New York City, this stretch of river
remains as unspoiled as it was in the early nineteenth century when Karl Baedeker, the German travel-book pub-
lisher, called it "finer than the Rhine."

Today the survival of this stretch in its unspoiled state is
trembling in the balance. The Consolidated Edison Company, in need of more electric-generating capacity to serve
the growing metropolitan area, has requested Government
permission to put a storage reservoir either on top of Storm
King, or close by, and to build a generating plant into the
side of the gorge. Whether it will be allowed to do this is
now being decided by the Federal Power Commission in
Washington.

The Storm King case has significance for us all, for behind it lies the story of how we, the American people, are
ruining the landscape and destroying natural resources at a
dangerously accelerating rate. Two main "villains" are
involved.

[4] From "America the (Formerly) Beautiful," by James Nathan Miller,
roving editor. Reader's Digest. 94:179-81+. F. '69. Reprinted with permission
from the February 1969 Reader's Digest. Copyright 1969 by The Reader's
Digest Assn., Inc.

People as Villains

One is the incredible growth of the U.S. population, which is almost literally blotting out the land. On Long Island, so much of the land is now covered with concrete and houses that certain areas have to be fenced off for special sump pits, to collect rainwater and give it a chance to soak into the earth. In Wisconsin, it is estimated that each year 150 square miles of rural land are being plastered over with roads and houses.

New Jersey, the "Garden State," gives perhaps the best picture of where we are heading. Today it's the garden-apartment state, with 807 people per square mile—twice the population density of India. Tomorrow? It will be the "City of New Jersey"; the Regional Plan Association of New York estimates that between 1960 and 1985 the New York metropolitan area will have reached out and consumed as much *additional* undeveloped land as it has so far occupied in the 340 years since the purchase of Manhattan from the Indians. In 1960 there were 113 million people in our urban areas; by the year 2000 there will likely be 280 million.

Consumer Demands on the Land

Superimpose on this population growth the enormous increase in the demands that each person is putting on the land. In electricity, for instance, the average American home is expected to increase its consumption some $2\frac{1}{2}$ times between 1960 and 1975. Thus we are already beginning to build dams and power plants on rivers that only a few years ago had seemed safe forever. The magnificent one-hundred-mile-long Hells Canyon on the Snake River on Idaho's western border, the deepest gorge in the United States, is now under threat of partial flooding by a big hydroelectric dam.

Or take the increased demand for road space. The 41,000-mile Interstate Highway System now being built, with an additional several hundred miles still under consideration, threatens redwood forests, and sweeps through suburban lawns and parks in many places. Yet it is only 65 per cent built, and when it is completed it will almost certainly be inadequate to our surging traffic needs as we continue to produce twice as many cars as babies and become a nation of two-car, even three-car, families.

To run these cars we need more oil. Thus, on the Banana River in Florida, and on Narragansett, Delaware and San Francisco bays, local citizens now have to fight to keep oil companies and other industries from building docks and refineries in the estuaries where fish and game birds have rested and bred for centuries. The Bureau of Sport Fisheries and Wildlife estimates that by 1980, the Connecticut shore-line—a vital stretch of the great Atlantic flyway—will have virtually no salt marsh suitable for wildfowl.

The Environmental Villains

The second villain of the piece: the Government agencies assigned to manage our resources. The best way to save Storm King, for example, is to persuade the FPC [Federal Power Commission] to refuse a construction license. But this is a dim hope. Indeed, four years ago in its first decision on Storm King—before conservationists appealed to the courts—the FPC unhesitatingly gave Consolidated Edison a go-ahead to build. For in the Commission's mind, if a plant is economically and technically sound, it is justified. Only once in its forty-four-year history has the FPC denied a power-plant application on esthetic grounds.

That, then, is the crux of the matter: the narrowness of view we have assigned to the Government agencies involved. We are managing our resources like a department store; we have appointed dozens of managers for the individual departments—electricity department, road department, flood-control department, irrigation department, forest department—but nobody is watching the store as a whole. The result is a chain reaction of narrow-interest decisions that block any overall look at what we are doing to the land.

In planning the route for a new road, for instance, state-highway engineers think mainly in terms of "user-benefits" —how many times a truck will have to shift gears on a hill, or the ton-mile cost to move a cargo from Point A to Point B. Scenic resources and local desires are rarely part of the equation.

The Tennessee Valley Authority has among its assignments the production of the cheapest possible electricity for its area. So it is forced to get half the coal for its power plants from companies that practice strip-mining—the cheapest but also the most destructive method. Gigantic power shovels leave exposed great white lumpy deserts of substrata called spoil banks which, because of their high acidity, are extremely difficult—sometimes impossible—to reclaim with tree plantings.

Narrow-interest agencies frequently become such fervid publicists of their own particular view of how to handle the land that all objectivity is lost. For instance, for years the Fish and Wildlife Service (in the Interior Department) promoted the sale of duck stamps to buy new duck-nesting areas and flood them. Simultaneously, the Agriculture Department, through special payments to farmers, was causing marshes to be drained at a far greater rate.

The Park Service (Interior Department) has developed a hard-sell pitch to local chambers of commerce aimed at taking land away from the Forest Service (Agriculture Department). The pitch: forest land does your community little economic good, but a park will bring tourists and dollars. The Soil Conservation Service (Agriculture), Army Engineers (Defense) and Bureau of Reclamation (Interior) all have elaborate competitive presentations on "how to get the Federal Government to build you a better watershed."

And lined up behind each of these agencies is a powerful group of private "clients," whose lobbies fight hard and effectively to perpetuate the rivalries. Behind the FPC are the advocates of private power; behind Reclamation and TVA are the public-power supporters. Behind the state-road departments are the trucking, road-building and gas-and-oil lobbies; and behind the United States Army Corps of Engineers is the most powerful lobby of all—the huge dam- and harbor-building contractors.

What Price for the Intangible?

What happens when the conservationists try to intervene and bring order to the process of resource management? They are swamped by an imposing stack of "user-benefit" formulas and "cost-benefit" ratios that invariably "prove" that the new road—or harbor or power plant or dam—serves the public interest.

Can "public interest" be completely defined in dollars-and-cents terms? Of course not. But this is precisely what we are trying to do—to put a price on the priceless values of beauty, relaxation, historical significance, wildlife.

In the process, we are destroying these intangibles faster than in nineteenth century robber-baron days. Soon, possibly in ten or fifteen years, we may wake up and realize that we have ruined our great national heritage.

Should we, then, stop building roads and dams and harbors? Certainly not. We will continue to prosper only as our economy expands. This will inevitably involve hard sacrifices of precious natural areas. What *we must* do is put an end to the present wasteful kind of helter-skelter, hit-or-miss expansion.

Conservationists ask two things, specifically:

1. That we give more weight to the nonmonetary considerations. Is it necessary, they ask, that a country as rich as ours give up an unspoiled Storm King Mountain or stretch of Hells Canyon, or sacrifice an irreplaceable grove of redwoods, in order to save a fraction of a per cent in the cost of electricity or in a truck's gas and tire bills?

2. That, when a road must be built or a valley flooded, we make sure that the best possible, least damaging site has been chosen. Today there is no such assurance.

Some hope stems from a court decision in the Storm King case—a decision that may still save the mountain. When conservationists took the case to court, on December 29, 1965, the United States Court of Appeals in New York issued a powerful statement: "In our affluent society, the cost of a project is only one of several factors to be considered"; the Commission should also take an "active and affirmative" look at the intangible cost. The court ordered the FPC to rehear the case and to bring to the hearings a totally new perspective: "a basic concern for the preservation of natural beauty and of national historic shrines."

Legal authorities believe that this decision may be a landmark in Federal regulation of natural resources. Indeed, it has already forced Consolidated Edison to make important concessions in the plant's design.

Even more needed is legislative reform to bring coordination to the conflicting agencies. For if the Engineers propagandize for dredging and damming instead of building irrigation systems, and the Bureau of Reclamation vice versa, it is because such are their assignments. You can't put a man in a position where his career depends on doing one thing, and expect him to recommend doing something else.

A bill before Congress, sponsored by Senator George McGovern [Democrat] of South Dakota, would create a high-level Council of Resource and Conservation Advisers to the President. The Council would be made up of three presidentially appointed resources experts without bureaucratic ties; dominated by no one interest, it would provide a *balanced* overall view of what we are doing with the land, air and water. The bill would also create in Congress two select committees on natural resources, made up of members of the four separate committees in each house that now consider resource matters. Unfortunately, opposed by strong lobbies and vested bureaucracies, this bill has little chance of passage at present. [Nixon signed a similar bill January 1, 1970. See "Establishment of Council of Environmental Advisers" in Section V, below.—Ed.]

But the need for such action grows daily. For unless we stop managing our resources in the present fragmentized way, we will soon run out of things worth fighting to keep.

OUR GROWING TRASH HEAPS [5]

Our environment is what's around us, and in the 1960s more American people became aware that much of what's around us is physically dangerous and esthetically unpleasant. In the decade ahead, we can expect a host of innovations in environmental control, but authorities predict that conditions will get worse before they get better.

The decade just ending has been the most productive that this nation or any nation has ever known, and this unexampled affluence has had a remarkable psychological impact upon Americans: They have become accustomed to throwing things away. It is the central fact of the U.S. environment today that the more the nation acquires in products and conveniences, the more difficult and complicated is the problem of disposing of unwanted materials.

The popular concept of environmental pollution includes the smokestack, the automobile exhaust pipe, and the dumping of industrial wastes at the river's edge. But the problem is larger and infinitely more complicated.

Consider rats. Why do rats prefer neighborhoods, city or rural, where poorer and less educated people live? A building that is old or in disrepair does not automatically attract rats. But "air-mailing" does. Air-mailing is the term given to one kind of casual removal of household garbage. An official of the United States Public Health Service (PHS) explains that it is common practice in slum tenements, for example, to fling chicken bones, vegetable peelings, and other kitchen waste out the window. The stuff lands on fire escapes, in alleys, and on the sidewalks, producing both a health hazard and a banquet for rodents. More than 14,000 rat bites are reported in the United States every year.

[5] "Struggling to Control Growing Trash Heaps," by Edwin A. Roberts, Jr. *National Observer*. p 18+. Ag. 18, '69. Reprinted by permission.

Such sloppiness is not restricted to the poor. A middle-income motorist might find one day that his automobile is sick beyond healing. The motorist may also find that it will cost him $30 to have his vehicle towed to a junkyard where it will bring $10 for scrap. The arithmetic is decisive. The motorist may remove the license plates and other identification and abandon the car on the street. In a month, or perhaps two, the municipality will spend the necessary money to tow the crate away.

Hospitals have a particularly sensitive waste problem. Linens can be boiled and laundered. Paper waste can be burned. But what of the disposable hypodermic needles that wind up in the trash can? If they are carted to the city dump along with other refuse, they become an acute health hazard to the workers who tend to the dumping. Thus the Bureau of Solid Wastes Management of the Public Health Service urges hospitals to place germ-laden needles in containers before they are tossed in the garbage can. But the bureau can only urge; there is no Federal law to back up such suggestions.

Says Richard D. Vaughan, director of the Bureau of Solid Wastes Management:

We've gotten good cooperation at the local level. State agencies are happy to work with the Public Health Service so long as they're sure we aren't trying to do their work for them, which we're not. Our job is to make recommendations based on our research and persuade the states and local bodies to take action on their own.

Some of Public Health's successes are based on simple ingenuity. Mr. Vaughan tells the story about an environmental problem in rural Alabama. In a certain area local residents had long been dumping refuse at fifteen different locations, creating fifteen small, unsanitary dumps. It's not easy to change the ways of country folk, so Mr. Vaughan's office didn't try. Instead, the Public Health Service, working with local officials, created a sanitary landfill at a central point among the fifteen small dumping spots. Large trash cans were then placed at each old dump. Local residents continued to cart their trash to the usual places, but now they put the waste in the cans. Municipal trucks regularly make the rounds of the fifteen dumping spots and haul all the refuse to the central sanitary-landfill dump.

If these examples of waste-disposal problems seem petty, they nevertheless add up to a huge national problem.

I sometimes don't understand Americans [says Mr. Vaughan]. In Europe you almost never see anyone discard anything in the street. In the United States I've seen "Don't Litter" signs practically covered with litter. Americans are litterers. The problem is so bad that we have sociologists working on the problem, trying to find out why Americans have such an untidy streak.

Every year [says a PHS spokesman], we generate 1.5 billion tons of animal wastes, 1.1 billion tons of mineral wastes, 550 million tons of agricultural waste and crop residues, 250 million tons of household, commercial, and municipal wastes, and 110 million tons of industrial wastes—a total of 3.5 billion tons of discards per year—and growing. Nonreturnable bottles, aluminum cans, and new types of disposable paper products complicate the problem.

And the cost continues to mount. Collection and disposal of garbage and other solid wastes cost taxpayers $3.5 billion in 1967, the latest year for which a reliable estimate is available, and the methods used are essentially the same as those of twenty-five years ago. Those methods are both mechanically primitive and hazardous to the public health.

Only 6 per cent of the nation's 12,000 land disposal sites "meet even less than minimum standards for sanitary landfills," says a PHS spokesman. Of the three hundred incinerators in the United States, 70 per cent are without adequate air pollution control systems.

The New Packaging

Trash has increased not only along with the population increase, but on a per capita basis too. Individual Americans discard more than their parents did, largely because so many things today come in packages and the packages themselves are being made of materials that don't decompose quickly.

New and ingenious packages are so popular and so convenient that we must find a way to dispose of them.

Consider beer. Years ago a man would go to his friendly neighborhood tavern with a pail that the barkeep would fill with draft beer. The beer was consumed and the pail reused. Today beer comes in glass bottles and aluminum cans. A discarded aluminum beer can cast on the side of a road will withstand the elements for thirty, perhaps fifty, years.

It would be far better, say PHS systems analysts, if beverages were sold in cardboard containers designed to withstand the pressure of their contents. It would be a help too if all glass bottles were returnable for reuse.

Instead, the trend to more durable packaging materials is likely to continue into the 1970s, even as major cities run out of dumping room. If Americans want the convenience of modern packaging, and if industry is more than willing to provide it, is the outlook completely hopeless?

No. Mr. Vaughan of the Bureau of Solid Wastes Management believes that industry has a responsibility for the final disposal of its products. He says the day is coming when, for instance, the automobile makers will have to participate in the handling of junked cars.

As for packaging, PHS scientists are working on new concepts of trash retrieval. Mr. Vaughan believes that in ten to fifteen years, all but 5 or 10 per cent of household garbage will be reclaimed.

It would be nice [he says], "if the American housewife could be persuaded to sort out garbage into fifteen different piles. Then all the plastic bottles and aluminum cans could be gathered and melted down for reuse. Well, my wife isn't about to take on such a job of garbage sorting and I doubt that many other wives would.

The answer lies in automation, in machinery that would automatically sort out trash, thus making it economic to reclaim not only plastics and metals but also food scraps that could be processed into fertilizer or for some other use.

This "recycling" of materials is necessary not only because present disposal methods are inherently wasteful and expensive. They are also increasingly dangerous as more sophisticated packaging materials come on the market. Many of those plastic bottles that can be bounced off the bathroom floor without breaking become a problem when they are incinerated. In burning, certain kinds of plastic give off a toxic gas that, among other things, peels the paint off buildings in the neighborhood.

The PHS uses three criteria to judge a sanitary-landfill dump: There should never be any burning at the dump (this causes air pollution); each day's deposit of garbage should be immediately buried; and the dump should be so engineered that there is no danger of polluting underground water.

Until a year ago, the dump rated as the very worst in the United States was operated in the District of Columbia just four miles from the Capitol. Congressmen sometimes wondered why Capitol Hill, when the wind was right (or wrong), was often enveloped in thick, odorous clouds of smoke. Today the fires are out at the notorious Kenilworth Dump, and a landfill system is used that soon will have converted the place into a park. A modern incinerator will then take care of the District's garbage.

One comes away from talks with the Public Health Service's solid-wastes experts feeling optimistic about America's chances of not being buried under an avalanche of garbage by the end of the 1970s, even though packaging consumption is expected to be 50 per cent greater in 1976 than it was in 1966. The Bureau of Solid Wastes Management has been in existence only three years, which indicates how late the size of the problem was recognized by Congress, but already the agency has worked with states, municipalities, and industry to advance both the sense of urgency and the necessary technology for dealing with waste materials.

The problem of polluted water, however, seems more complicated, partly for scientific reasons and partly because of jurisdictional uncertainties.

Pollution is a relative term, and water experts say the American people must decide not only that they want clean rivers and streams, but how clean they want them. Water, for example, can be clean enough to bathe in but dangerous to drink. Such water might also be hazardous to fish life. [See "Toward a Water Pollution Policy," in Section III, above.]

There are many causes of water pollution, and some are much more difficult to control than others. Present technology is capable of eliminating pollution caused by the runoff of such chemicals as those in fertilizers. This runoff stimulates the growth of algae in the water. During the daytime, the algae, as do other plants, absorb carbon dioxide and give off oxygen, which is fine. But the bacteria that flourish in an algae-heavy stream give off carbon dioxide day and night, more than the algae can handle because the photosynthesis mechanism in algae shuts down at night.

The result is a progressive loss of oxygen in the water. Lake Erie is a good example of this kind of pollution, which results in dead fish and water that smells and tastes bad. [See "Lake Erie: A Dying Lake," in Section III, above.] Such water is, in fact, toxic and can cause paralytic shellfish poisoning. When algae get out of control in farm pounds, livestock are in jeopardy.

The technique for ridding a body of water of this kind of pollution is called "mixing the lake." Bottom water is pumped to the surface to overcome what scientists call "thermal stratification." The technique works very well, but must be repeated every summer.

A more difficult pollution problem is that caused by the pouring of slaughterhouse wastes into waterways. These wastes produce ammonia nitrogen that also reduces the water's oxygen content. The currently favored method of approaching this nuisance is with an alkaline treatment that gets rid of the ammonia, but scientists say research is continuing to find more efficient techniques.

Just about everybody connected with water pollution seems convinced that the nation can have clean water only if there is more Federal spending for research combined with tax incentives to industry to encourage better waste processing.

There are few Americans who haven't seen, felt, and smelled polluted air. There are days in Los Angeles, New York, and other cities when human beings are affected almost as by tear gas. And although we tend to think of air pollution as an evil of our modern industrial society, the problem is hardly new.

In the Bible there is this passage: ". . . and from the shaft rose smoke, like the smoke of a great furnace, and the sun and the air were darkened with the smoke from the shaft. . . . By these three plagues a third of mankind was killed, by the fire and smoke and sulphur issuing from their mouths." (Revelation 9:2 and 18.)

Death to Polluters

Dr. Glenn T. Seaborg, chairman of the United States Atomic Energy Commission, recently noted that there have been many attempts throughout history to legislate against the causes of air pollution: "One of the first laws against air pollution was recorded earlier than 1300, when King Edward I (1239-1307) issued an edict against the burning of coal. The penalty was death—and history records at least one execution for this offense."

This writer recalls the remark of a Soviet journalist who took him for a boat ride on the Volga River. Directly in front of a huge steel plant, people were fishing and swimming in remarkably clean water. I asked the journalist how the river could be kept so clean. He held up an empty bottle and replied: "If I throw this bottle into the river, I will likely go to jail for six months."

Similarly, the air around the steel plant was free of pollution, owing partly to stringent controls on smoke output and partly to the installation of electric furnaces.

With much of industry committed to the effort, it's likely that dramatic progress in air pollution control will be made

in the United States in the decade ahead. New autos will
spew forth less carbon monoxide because the internal-com-
bustion engine will be made more efficient, or possibly because steam-powered and electric cars will become economic.
[See "Antipollution and the Electric Car" and "Automobiles
and Antipollution Measures," in Section II, above.] New
filtering systems in factories and the increased use of nuclear
power and fossil fuels with a lower sulfur content are also
part of the answer.

Another environmental problem that worries specialists
is radiological pollution. Chris A. Hansen, assistant surgeon
general and the commissioner of the Environmental Control
Administration, makes the point this way:

Let's just say that it could be shown that a child sitting a
certain distance from the front of a color television set would not
be adversely affected by radiation if he sat in that spot for five
hours a day for ten years. But what if it were necessary for that
same child, after all that exposure to color-TV radiation, to have
X rays taken? The total radiation buildup in that case could well
be something to worry about.

Another potential source of radiation danger is the electronic cooking oven. Add to this such "outside" sources of
radioactivity as nuclear fallout (some radioactive material
from past atomic explosions still is drifting down from high
in the atmosphere) and the twenty-five to thirty new nu-
clear-reactor installations being built each year, and the
grand total of radioactivity around us is not insignificant.
The important point is that in the decade ahead, radiation
hazards will multiply unless new controls prove workable.

The new controls were authorized by the Radiation Control for Health and Safety Act of 1968, which directs the
Secretary of Health, Education, and Welfare to "establish
and carry out an electronic-product radiation-control program designed to protect the public health and safety from
electronic-product radiation."

Specifically, manufacturers must report to the Government any defect in a product that could expose the public

to radiation dangers. Importers of electronic products are subject to a similar rule. Most importantly, the Environmental Control Administration was directed to come up with standards that manufacturers would have to meet before their electronic products could be sold, if such standards were considered necessary for a particular product.

When people think of environmental problems, they generally think in terms of the outdoors. But our environment certainly includes the buildings in which we work. The environmental dangers for many workers are mounting rapidly.

Government specialists say that the average worker is off the job for nearly six days and experiences more than sixteen days of restricted activity annually because of occupational injury or illness. The cost to the nation is $60 billion a year. The problem is likely to get worse as technology becomes more complex.

It's estimated that every twenty minutes a new and potentially toxic chemical is introduced into industry. "Yet," says a PHS [Public Health Service] spokesman, "adequate documentation exists for only 400 of the 12,000 potentially toxic chemicals in current use. New technology in the form of tools as powerful as the laser introduce potential hazards. And an estimated 7 million industrial workers are exposed in the workplace to noise levels that could damage hearing."

The Environmental Control Administration, in a list of "damaging or distracting noises," places rock 'n' roll bands in the same sentence with sonic booms and highway traffic.

American industry is aware of the work-environment hazards and spends $320 million a year on plant safety. Unfortunately, only 20 per cent of the nation's 80 million workers are covered by such services, which may be why workmen's compensation payments to occupationally disabled workers exceed $2.2 billion and are going up every year.

In the 1970s, safety programs will be expanded, but it remains a question whether preventive systems can keep up with the multiplying hazards that are part of industrial progress.

These then are the principal environmental problems that face the nation today and promise to be around in the 1970s.

There are also more general problems—problems relating to the changing role of the cities and their gradual deterioration as businesses decentralize and middle-class families show little interest in returning to urban neighborhoods.

Scholars at the University of Minnesota and elsewhere are working on the design of totally new experimental cities, cities that would be built in places where today there is only countryside. Such mammoth projects would incorporate all that man has learned about urban systems since the nation's older cities were founded.

Seeing the Total Picture

The United States has plenty of space for such experiments. Major cities and their suburban satellites account for only a tiny fraction of America's land area. But erecting new cities, and even the successful reclaiming of old cities, require the cooperative efforts of government on many levels, and such cooperation is not easily achieved, to say nothing of getting people to live in wide-open spaces.

But even as new approaches to environmental problems are dreamed up, and even as those problems are further complicated by a growing population and an accelerating technology, it's probably wise to keep the total picture in mind.

If environment refers to what's around us, then our environment also includes the awesome coast of Oregon, the sparkling desert nights in southern Arizona, the Everglades glowing red in the summer dawn, the waltzing wheatfields of Kansas, the New York City skyline at dusk, the luxurious cabin of a jet airliner, air-conditioned autos and broad turnpikes and winding parkways, the pretty clothes of American women, and the laughter of children.

Nevertheless, we may hope that in the next decade. Americans will begin to take better care of the environment, to make national cleanliness a national goal. Garbage tossed out of windows, old cars abandoned on city streets, industrial carelessness about waste disposal—these kinds of pollution are infuriating.

Reflecting on such sloppiness, this reporter could only feel anger as he emerged from the handsome new headquarters of the Environmental Control Administration in Rockville, Maryland. His anger was such, in fact, that he didn't even realize he was tapping out his pipe ashes on the front steps of the building.

ELIMINATING ALL WASTE [6]

If you think splitting the atom and harnessing its power was incredible, if you think putting men on the moon is fantastic, let me tell you about something two Atomic Energy Commission scientists are working on that can only be called apocalyptic. They are working on a project to eliminate all waste! Yes, make this a wasteless world! It sounds like the millennium.

Did you know that each person in the United States produces 4.8 pounds per day of solid waste? That by the year 2000 each person will produce 6.8 pounds per day? That over the thirty-five-year period from 1965 to 2000 almost 10 billion tons of solid refuse will have been accumulated in the United States?

If this were all compacted and disposed of in sanitary landfill, it would cover the state of Delaware ten feet deep! It would cover the state of Rhode Island twenty feet deep! At the cost of $1 a foot (the cost of sanitary landfill in Los Angeles), this layer of solid waste would represent a total investment of about half a trillion dollars!

To the solid wastes of municipal refuse has to be added the solid wastes of industrial origin—junked cars, waste material resulting from mining of solid fuels, metals. The man-

[6] From "Project Seeks to Eliminate All Waste," by Neal Stanford, staff correspondent. *Christian Science Monitor.* p 7. O. 23, '69. Reprinted by permission from *The Christian Science Monitor.* © 1969 The Christian Science Publishing Society. All rights reserved.

agement of waste materials, or, better, its elimination, would quite obviously be an unparalleled boon to mankind. It would be the material equivalent of perpetual motion.

At the moment, the ability to create something from basic elements, use it as a product or service, and then economically reduce it back to its basic elements for future use (with no adverse effect on nature) sounds like fantasy. It smacks of alchemy. What it would mean to mankind staggers the imagination: a pollution-free world; a wasteless society; a control over matter such as man has never had.

The process involved in this concept is called "the fusion torch." It rests upon the prospect of man being able to tame the hydrogen—or fusion—bomb, just as he tamed the nuclear —or fission—bomb. Controlled atomic fission made possible nuclear reactors.

Controlled atomic fusion would not only allow man on a large scale and economic basis to desalt water, process urban sewage, perform plasma chemistry, produce electricity through fuel cells, but also to recycle essentially all solid waste.

That last operation constitutes the fusion-torch concept, or closing the cycle from use to reuse. What this means in layman's language is that waste products would be converted back to elemental form. There would be no waste products to dispose of. There would rather be a supply of basic raw materials for reuse.

When fusion reactors become available, a volume of materials equal to thousands of tons per day could be handled in a single plant. That would take care of urban waste even in the volume produced today. It is said that if just 10,000 megawatts were used for processing via the fusion torch, the entire wastes of a city with a population in the millions could be converted into raw materials each day.

Who are these modern Merlins—the men working to make possible a wasteless world? Drs. Bernard J. Eastlund and William C. Gough, of the AEC's [Atomic Energy Commission] division of research, as well as the many scientists, physicists, and engineers working on the problem of controlled thermonuclear fusion.

It can be reported that at present new progress has been made both in the United States and in the Soviet Union in this field. The Soviets, it is understood, have made particularly great strikes recently.

Ultimate Solution?

In this matter of waste management, two possibilities exist today. Now the fusion-torch concept provides the third —or ultimate—solution. Waste disposal produces no economic return. Partial recycle involves some economic penalty. But this prospect of closing the cycle of use of a resource back to resource makes waste itself a resource.

The fusion-torch concept is a bit complicated for the layman, so it may be better to let the nuclear scientists working on it explain it in their own words.

This is how Drs. Eastlund and Gough describe their fusion-torch concept:

> This closing the basic link from user back to resource would be accomplished by vaporizing and ionizing solids (for example, ores or waste products) in the plasma and then separating the elements from the mixture of ionized species.
>
> A fusion plasma is able to vaporize solids easily by the propagation of shock waves. This is because of the plasma's tremendously large flux of random kinetic energy and its high thermal conductivity.

To control fusion energy say Drs. Eastlund and Gough, "we must heat a dilute gas of fusion fuel to temperatures of hundreds of millions of degrees, then contain it long enough (and at sufficient purity) for an appreciable fraction of the fuel to react." That first goal, they say, was achieved five years ago when plasmas above the ideal ignition temperature were obtained for a self-sustaining fusion reactor. So the problem now is to confine the hot plasmas.

These two scientists say that progress to this end "has been accelerating as the result of increased correlation between theory and experiment, also the use of advanced computers for plasma simulation."

They become quite enthusiastic in explaining their fusion-torch concept:

The fusion torch would close the basic link from user back to resource. Waste products would be converted back to elemental form.

When a solid is injected into the fusion torch, the interaction results in the transformation of an ultrahigh temperature hydrogen plasma into a low-temperature plasma composed of ionic species characteristic of the solid, irrespective of a solid's chemical composition of mechanical properties.

The number of processes needed for complete recovery of elements from waste products would equal the number of types of waste products present. The fusion torch probably would handle all species in one central recovery plant.

Drs. Eastlund and Gough, while immersed in their research on fusion and on fusion-torch physics, certainly have a vision, a vision, as they put it,

of the future—large cities, operated electrically by clean, safe fusion reactors that eliminate the city's waste products and generate the city's raw materials. . . .

The vision is there. Its attainment does not appear to be blocked by nature. Its achievement depends on the will and the desire of men to see that it is brought about.

V. WHAT CAN BE DONE?

EDITOR'S INTRODUCTION

Political, economic, and scientific measures that might be employed to combat air pollution and the fouling of our waterways and natural landscape have been noted throughout this compilation. What follows in this last section refers to certain other measures that have been taken here and abroad with new suggestions which may be acted on. It is for the reader to judge whether the actions and measures recommended appear adequate to deal with the dire threats to the environment and to human life which were outlined in Section I.

The first short statements below outline from an official viewpoint the Federal activities dealing with environmental problems which are now carried out from Washington. Next a reporter for *Science,* Luther J. Carter, gives a critique of the new Environment Quality Council, a Cabinet-level agency created in 1969 by President Richard M. Nixon. This is followed by a consideration of a plan proposing the creation of educational institutions to deal with environmental problems analagous to the agricultural land-grant universities established by the Federal Government in the latter part of the nineteenth century.

Can taxation of polluters be a partial answer to our environmental problems? And, in any case, what in aggregate may be the cost of cleaning up pollution in our nation as a whole? These two questions are dealt with in an article by Irston R. Barnes of the Washington *Post* and a lecture by Charles Sackrey, an economist at Smith College. Following these the editor of a national legal magazine, *Trial,* indicates that only through swift legal action against polluters will we begin to see quick results in pollution abatement.

Early in January 1970, President Nixon made clear that
the Federal Government would take a more active role in
antipollution efforts. On January 1, he approved the National Environmental Policy Act which creates a three-member Council of Environmental Advisers comparable to the
President's Council of Economic Advisers. The President's
statement on approving this action is included below. Later,
in his State of the Union Message to Congress on January 22,
Mr. Nixon urged that a "war on pollution" be undertaken
in the decade of the seventies to improve the condition of
America's environment.

The last two articles refer first to action taken in Sweden,
which has now embarked on a comprehensive antipollution
program, and then to action to be taken by the United Nations respecting environmental problems—action sparked by
the initiative of Sweden.

CONSUMERS AND HEALTH SERVICES [1]

Today our nation is faced with an environmental crisis
which is recognized as one of the major problems of our time.
Urbanization, a soaring population, fantastic advances in
technology, and the mistakes of the past have produced biological, radiological and chemical contamination of land, air,
food, and water; crowding; noise; destruction of natural resources; and many other threats to human health and well-
being.

We have been guilty of collective failure to foresee the
unwanted byproducts of progress. Many diverse human activities have contributed to the deterioration of the environment. Now various aspects of the problem increasingly engage, and must engage, the attention of interest groups in
many diverse fields—conservation, agriculture, transporta-

[1] "The Consumer Protection and Environmental Health Service," intro-
duction, by Charles C. Johnson, Jr., assistant surgeon general, administrator in
Public Health Service. In pamphlet, *The Consumer Protection and Environ-
mental Health Service.* (Public Health Service Publication no 1872) United
States. Department of Health, Education, and Welfare. Public Health Service.
Washington, D.C. 20201. '68. p 1-4.

tion, urban planning, industry, commerce, health, consumer protection, and others.

As environmental change has accelerated, it has become more and more apparent that we must learn to make sound judgments as to what is, or is not, a permissible or desirable alteration in the environment. *Clearly, the considerations forming the basis for such judgments must focus on human health and welfare.*

The Consumer Protection and Environmental Health Service has been established to help our nation achieve a deeper insight into the relationship of man to his environment, to assess the total impact on the human organism of the many diverse environmental stresses which simultaneously impinge on modern man, and to provide criteria by which our nation may evaluate its diverse activities which affect the consumer and his environment.

There are three aspects of the human environment, although it is not possible, in reality, to separate them: the environment of air, water, and land; the environment of home, work, school, and recreation; and the environment of the products and services we consume or use.

Although science has long recognized that all the factors, benign or malignant, which man encounters in all these facets of the environment combine to produce a total effect on his physical and mental health, we have too long attempted to deal with them as though their effects were, in fact, separate and unrelated. Indeed, we have sometimes seemed to view man as outside the ecological system and to deal with various factors in the environment as though they were merely problems of planetary property management. In truth, man, whatever else he may be, is a part of nature, whose life is dependent upon a delicate balance within the ecological system of which he is a part.

The Department of Health, Education, and Welfare, as the agency primarily concerned with the health and well-being of the whole population, has charged the Consumer Protection and Environmental Health Service with assuring that human environmental needs are defined and enunciated as clearly as possible so that consideration of man's health and welfare may become a guiding principle, throughout our society, in all actions affecting the environment. The new Service is concerned with the whole spectrum of environmental and consumer hazards and brings together, in a relationship in which they can be mutually supportive, the principal activities of the Department of Health, Education, and Welfare which deal with these problems. Within it are three operating agencies: the Food and Drug Administration, the National Air Pollution Control Administration, and the Environmental Control Administration.

In discharging its mission, the Service will:

1. Determine the influence of the contemporary environment on man's health and welfare by consolidating and evaluating existing knowledge, and advance, through research, our understanding of the impact of environmental change on man

2. Develop broad criteria and, when appropriate, establish standards specifying permissible levels of human exposure to environmental impacts

3. Exercise fully the several regulatory authorities vested in it and, if necessary to the accomplishment of its mission, seek appropriate additional authority

4. Assist industry and government at all levels by promoting the development, improvement, and application of techniques to eliminate, control, or prevent environmental hazards

5. Help state and local jurisdictions develop broad, effective environmental and consumer protection programs through such means as demonstration projects, manpower development programs, and financial, technical, and planning assistance

A national effort, involving every segment of our society, will be required to achieve an environment truly suitable to human needs. Our work will help to define and illuminate many difficult problems for all those, in both the public and private sectors, whose daily decisions determine the quality of the environment in which we, and future generations, will live.

FOOD AND DRUG SERVICES [2]

The Food and Drug Administration [FDA] is responsible for assuring that foods are safe, pure and wholesome; that drugs and therapeutic devices are safe and effective; that cosmetics are safe; and that all these are honestly and informatively labeled and packaged. In addition, it has broad responsibilities in other areas of consumer protection: hazardous substances, poisons, and pesticides, as well as other products which may present hazards to the user.

FDA carries out a continuing surveillance program to protect the consumer from adulterated, contaminated, or misbranded foods. It determines the safety of food additives before approving their use and establishes safe levels for pesticide residues on food. Through research, it expands and updates scientific knowledge of potential health hazards, particularly those associated with new food technology. The agency encourages self-regulation by the food industry. . . .

The safety and effectiveness of all drugs shipped in interstate commerce—both prescription and over-the-counter products—are FDA's concern. The agency monitors clinical tests of new drugs and requires drug manufacturers to provide evidence that new drugs are safe and effective for their intended use before they can be sold. After a drug is placed on the market, the manufacturer must report to FDA any unexpected side effects; FDA itself collects other reports of experience with the drug. A comprehensive program to maintain quality controls includes plant inspections, continuing tests at the National Center for Drug Analysis, and industry educational activities to promote good manufactur-

[2] From "Food and Drug Administration," by Herbert L. Ley, Jr., M.D., former commissioner, United States Department of Health, Education, and Welfare. In pamphlet, *The Consumer Protection and Environmental Health Service.* (Public Health Service Publication no 1872) United States. Department of Health, Education, and Welfare. Public Health Service. Washington, D.C. 20201. '68. p 5-7.

ing practices. The goal is voluntary compliance with Federal law and regulations, supported by consistent enforcement action when required.

Cosmetics are required by law to be free of substances that may be injurious, to be produced in a sanitary plant, packaged in a safe and nondeceptive container, and honestly and completely labeled. FDA may remove from interstate commerce any cosmetic shown to be unsafe, adulterated, or misbranded.

The law requires that medical devices must be safe and effective when used as directed. Sellers of devices which are harmful, or which will not perform as claimed, may be prosecuted and their products seized. In the past, FDA has directed its attention primarily to quackery and fraud. Today, however, such new and useful devices as pacemakers, artificial kidneys, and iron lungs are common tools of health care, and advancements in medical engineering offer an exciting prospect for the future. FDA is responsible for assuring . . . that such devices are of uniformly high quality.

FDA supports the operation of a national poison control network to facilitate diagnosis and treatment of poison victims; it enforces labeling requirements covering hazardous substances and, under some circumstances, may ban such products from the market; it studies hazards in pesticide use and is the principal Federal adviser on the health aspects of pesticides; it seeks to identify and control hazards to the consumer from products purchased on the open market.

AIR POLLUTION CONTROL ADMINISTRATION [3]

The National Air Pollution Control Administration conducts a comprehensive program of research and training,

[3] "National Air Pollution Control Administration," by John T. Middleton, commissioner, United States Department of Health, Education, and Welfare. In pamphlet, *The Consumer Protection and Environmental Health Service.* (Public Health Service Publication no 1872) United States. Department of Health, Education, and Welfare. Public Health Service. Washington, D.C. 20201. '68. p 8-9.

financial and technical assistance to state and local agencies, and abatement and control activities to help protect the American people from the harmful effects of air pollution. The Administration's activities are aimed specifically at increasing knowledge of the nature, source, effects, and control of air pollution and at achieving maximum application of this knowledge.

Under the Air Quality Act of 1967, the Administration has initiated new efforts to achieve effective air pollution control on a regional basis. Air pollution problem areas are being designated as air quality control regions. At the same time, the Administration is developing and will publish air quality criteria describing the known effects of air pollution on health and welfare. Together with the criteria, the Administration will publish information on techniques for controlling pollutants at their source. State governments will be expected to use the criteria and control-technology information as a basis for developing air quality standards for the regions and plans for implementing and enforcing the standards.

By the end of 1969, it is expected that air quality control regions will be designated in thirty-two of the nation's largest urban areas, whose inhabitants comprise about 64 per cent of our entire urban population. During this same period, air quality criteria and information on control technology for several of the most important pollutants will be made available.

The Administration awards grants and provides technical assistance to states, as well as local governments, to help them plan and carry on effective programs for the prevention and control of air pollution, not only in air quality control regions but also in other places where air pollution problems exist.

Through research, the Administration seeks to develop effective and economical methods for controlling or preventing the discharge of pollutants to the atmosphere and to gain improved knowledge of the effects of pollution on humans, plants, animals, and materials. Several other Federal agencies and an increasing number of industrial firms and other organizations in the private sector are participating in the Administration's research program.

The Administration also conducts a national regulatory program aimed at controlling pollution from motor vehicles. National standards for the control of pollution from new motor vehicles have been prescribed by the Secretary of DHEW [Department of Health Education, and Welfare]. Their application began with 1968 motor cars.

The Administration's manpower development activities include training courses for air pollution research and control personnel and support of graduate-level training through grants to universities and fellowships to individual students.

ENVIRONMENTAL CONTROL ADMINISTRATION [4]

The Environmental Control Administration conducts a broad national program to identify and control a wide range of problems relating to the environment in which modern man lives, works, and spends his leisure time. It is especially concerned with the multitude of environmental problems affecting urban populations.

It directs specific attention to such hazards as improper housing, noise, rodent and insect vectors, radiation, waste accumulation, improper sanitation, and occupational disease and injury, but is concerned as well with all other impacts on man's health and welfare that are associated with the

[4] "Environmental Control Administration," by Chris A. Hansen, commissioner, United States Department of Health, Education, and Welfare. In pamphlet, *The Consumer Protection and Environmental Health Service.* (Public Health Service Publication no 1872) United States. Department of Health, Education, and Welfare. Public Health Service. Washington, D.C. 20201. '68. p 10-12.

contemporary environment. It develops recommended codes and ordinances covering sanitary requirements.

It conducts and supports research and training; provides technical assistance; and offers demonstration and planning grants for solid waste management.

The Administration seeks workable solutions to the nation's growing problem of disposing of trash, garbage, and other solid wastes. It considers various possible approaches, including the recycling of wastes in the industries in which they are produced, control over disposable containers and packaging materials, and recovery of valuable resources from wastes.

It is concerned with existing and potential health surveillance of radiation in the environment, develops standards for radiation control, disseminates technical information, and cooperates with the states in planning, developing and evaluating control programs. An important phase of research is aimed at reducing unnecessary radiation exposure in the healing arts. The Administration also evaluates proposals to construct nuclear power plants from a public health standpoint. It is responsible for Federal regulation of radiation emissions from electronic products.

Its occupational health program is directed at protecting and improving the health of the nation's 80 million workers. Its scientists study the effects of dusts, chemicals, noise, and other occupational hazards on man, and develop and recommend preventive or control measures for application in industry.

The Administration seeks to improve the nation's health by assuring high quality water for domestic consumption, recreational use, the growing of shellfish, and other water resource uses affecting public health. It develops the official Public Health Service Drinking Water Standards, surveys and approves municipal water supply systems to serve as water sources for interstate carriers, and performs research and studies on long-range effects of chemical contaminants and other health problems related to water. A major function of the water supply program is to advise governmental and other agencies on health concerns related to water resource development, water uses, and water pollution.

The Administration cooperates with states in their milk sanitation programs and certifies the quality of milk shipped across state lines.

A CRITIQUE OF FEDERAL ACTION [5]

The "new conservation" concept that government and industry should take careful account of the impact of their activities on the total environment, viewed as a complex of intricately related natural systems, has come into high vogue in Washington in recent years. Even the United States Army Corps of Engineers, superintendent of the congressional pork barrel, has been hiring ecologists and promising to give a new emphasis to environmental studies in its project planning. Credit for spreading the gospel of the new conservation belongs in good part to the Kennedy and Johnson administrations and, more particularly, to their Secretary of the Interior, Stewart L. Udall. Now, it is up to the Nixon Administration to see if the Federal departments and agencies can be coaxed or goaded into actually living by the newly proclaimed faith.

Though vague in the abstract, this gospel has a meaning which conservationists find all too clear in situations where it has been ignored. They note, for example, that the Atomic Energy Commission is licensing nuclear-fired steam electric generating plants without due regard for the thermal pollution problems these plants may cause. Also, there is the plight of the Everglades National Park, which has been hurt by a Corps of Engineers flood control project in central Florida that has upset the park's hydraulic regime, and which is now threatened by a jetport being built nearby with the

[5] From "Environmental Quality: Nixon's New [Environment Quality] Council Raises Doubts," by Luther J. Carter, staff reporter. *Science.* 165:44-6. Jl. 4, '69. Copyright 1969 by the American Association for the Advancement of Science. Reprinted by permission.

help of grants from the Department of Transportation. [On
January 15, 1970, this threat was removed. The Nixon Administration announced an agreement with state and local
authorities in Florida forbidding construction of a major international jetport near the Everglades National Park.—Ed.]

And conservationists point, too, to the oil-smeared shores
of Santa Barbara Channel, where the Department of the
Interior's failure to ascertain the hazards of allowing drilling
into the oil-bearing formation lying only a few hundred feet
beneath the sea bottom contributed to the disastrous well
blowout there. Such examples of serious harm resulting from
failure to weigh the possible environmental consequences of
public and private undertakings are common, and threats to
natural areas are not all that is involved—instances of highway builders, urban renewal authorities, and private developers doing damage to "urban ecology" are numerous and
well-documented.

In his first major step in dealing with the problem of
environmental protection, President Nixon, on 29 May
[1969], issued an executive order establishing a new interagency Environment Quality Council, naming himself
chairman, Vice President Agnew as vice chairman, and Lee
A. DuBridge, his science adviser, as executive secretary. The
President said that the new council will review existing policies and programs, project the environmental impact of new
technologies, and "encourage scientific developments which
will help us protect our resources." "We have become victims of our own technological genius," Nixon said, though
adding that the new council would provide the strategy for
a "high quality of life" and the means to implement that
strategy.

The appointment of a new interagency council stirs
little excitement in Washington, for such bodies have been
numerous and their record of accomplishment has been
small. In fact, President Nixon's new council will replace
President Johnson's Council on Recreation and Natural
Beauty, a body of deservedly little renown. Such interagency

councils, though established in answer to problems felt to be important enough to demand the concerted attention of the Cabinet secretaries, generally have promised more than they have delivered because (1) Cabinet secretaries are too hard-pressed by other duties to regularly attend council meetings themselves; and (2) one secretary or agency head tends to overlook the mote in the eye of another, all knowing that in such mutual forbearance lies the best hope of escaping troublesome criticism. (President Johnson's science adviser, Donald F. Hornig, once told an interviewer that the Federal Council for Science and Technology, a subcabinet-level body which he chaired, had had some success in resolving conflicts between agencies; he said, however, that its members generally were unwilling to criticize each other's agency policies and programs.)

The shortcomings seemingly inherent in interagency councils were on the minds of the members of the Senate Interior Committee . . . when the committee was taking up the question of what kind of White House advisory apparatus on environmental policy would be best. Although the President had not yet set up his new council, he was planning to do so, and DuBridge appeared before the committee to explain how, this time, such a council really could be made to work.

According to DuBridge, President Nixon himself would preside over the council meetings, just as he was usually presiding over the Council of Urban Affairs which he established shortly after taking office.

This [urban affairs] council, too, is composed of Cabinet members, with the President as the active—and, I assure you—very vigorous and interested chairman [DuBridge said and added] . . . tasks can be assigned then and there to the proper Cabinet officer or to a group or committee of Cabinet officers. Things decided upon can be implemented instantly, by Presidential directive.

Secretary of the Interior Walter J. Hickel, the only member of the new council whose principal concern is environmental matters, also said he felt the council would be an effective policy-making mechanism. Despite these assurances, however, Senator Henry M. Jackson [Democrat] of Washington, chairman of the Interior Committee, and a number of other senators expressed skepticism. Senator Gaylord Nelson [Democrat] of Wisconsin, for example, told Hickel:

> Everybody here knows that there are three hundred hours of time demanded of the President for every hour that the poor man who holds that responsibility can give. In all due respect, the President is just too harassed. I just quite frankly don't think he can devote the necessary time to this problem.

This view was shared by Lynton K. Caldwell, professor of government at Indiana University and a committee witness, who observed that the nation was looking too much to the White House for leadership on too many issues. "The country is too big, the issues are too complex, to make this a realistic attitude," Caldwell said. "And we do not have yet, even in the President, a superman."

Democratic Views

Senator Edmund Muskie [Democrat] of Maine, chairman of the Senate Air and Water Pollution Subcommittee, takes a more positive view of the President's new council—provided it is supported by adequate staff work. He has introduced a bill, cosponsored by some forty senators, which would set up an Office of Environmental Quality in the executive office of the President. The director of this new office could be the President's science adviser, or someone else, whom the President chooses.

Senator Jackson, Muskie's rival claimant in the Senate for the title of Mr. Environment, has developed a proposal which, while not directly in conflict with the Muskie bill, takes a different approach. It would establish in the Office of the President a three-member council on environmental quality, a body which would be analogous to the council of economic advisers. In Jackson's concept, this would be a body of three wise men to whom the President and his interagency council could look for "independent and impartial" advice.

The Jackson bill, which former Secretary of the Interior Udall supports, also spells out a national policy encouraging a "productive and enjoyable harmony between man and his environment"; more than that, it would require that proposals for Federal projects be examined from the standpoint of their impact on the environment. The agencies concerned would have to certify, among other things, that any adverse environmental effects which cannot be avoided are "justified by stated considerations of national policy." According to an aide, Senator Jackson expects his measure to receive favorable Senate action this year. [See "Establishment of Council of Environmental Advisers," in Section V, below.]

In the House, Representative John Dingell [Democrat] of Detroit, chairman of the wildlife subcommittee of the Merchant Marine and Fisheries Committee, is sponsoring a bill similar to Jackson's. . . . Perennially, there are proposals to revamp the bureaucracy. [In 1969] Representative Emilio Q. Daddario [Democrat] of Connecticut, chairman of the science subcommittee of the Committee on Science and Astronautics . . . [sponsored] a bill to establish a Department of Resources, Environment, and Population. A key idea here is that, unless resources and population are kept in balance, conservation efforts are sure to fail. In the Senate, Frank Moss [Democrat] of Utah, Clifford Case [Republican] of New Jersey, and Mike Gravel [Democrat] of Alaska also are proposing the establishment of a new agency, theirs to be called the Department of Conservation and the Environment. The Department of the Interior would be abolished, with most of the bureaus now within it being absorbed by the new department. But units such as the Office of Oil and Gas and the Bureau of Commercial Fisheries would be transferred to the Department of Commerce. While this would relieve some of the conflicts now present within the Department of the Interior, it would obviously create new problems of coordination.

Political interest in the environmental-quality issue is such that it seems likely that, within the next year or so, legislation of some sort will be enacted in an effort to improve decision making in this field. According to Senator Jackson, there is now general agreement between him and the Nixon Administration on the need for his proposed council of environmental advisers. Actually, the Administration's attitude seems to be more one of acquiescence in the Jackson proposal than of wholehearted endorsement. There is, in fact, reason to think that the Muskie bill setting up an office to support the President's interagency council comes closer to the Administration's desires.

But whatever the nature of the new mechanisms which it may ultimately prescribe, Congress is putting the heat on the Administration to deliver on its promises to translate the "new conservation" from doctrine into practice.

EDUCATION FOR CONSERVATION [6]

A staff report from the White House Office of Science and Technology [OST] recommends that the Government encourage universities and colleges to establish multidisciplinary "schools of the human environment," which would be a kind of analog to the schools of agriculture and of public health which have proved so successful as problem-focused research and training endeavors. It proposes that about $20 million in Federal funds be provided initially to help interested institutions launch such programs or build upon efforts already under way—and it makes biting observations about purported multidisciplinary programs now supported by Federal agencies.

The report was released to the press on 5 November [1969] by Lee A. DuBridge, the President's science adviser, who, while not explicitly endorsing the document, said that

[6] From "Environmental Studies: OST [Office of Science and Technology] Report Urges Better Effort," by Luther J. Carter, staff reporter. *Science.* 166: 851. N. 14, '69. Copyright 1969 by the American Association for the Advancement of Science. Reprinted by permission.

it deserves serious consideration. It is to be taken up later this month at the next meeting of the Environmental Quality Council, the new Cabinet-level body over which President Nixon presides.

The report was prepared by John S. Steinhart, an OST staff member who specializes in environmental matters, and Miss Stacie Cherniack, a White House summer intern who is now a senior majoring in political science at the University of California at Berkeley. If one may judge from the force and clarity of this report, it would be desirable to have an undergraduate assist in the preparation of all Government documents.

The response to various funding programs of the Government in defense, space, and a variety of other areas has caused universities to erect a wide variety of institutes, centers, and programs to respond to available funds [the report said]. In most cases these institutes have been largely paper structures, and their impact on the universities and, especially, on the students and the public discussion of the issues surrounding the work has been negligible. Curriculum, faculty rewards, and most of the research have been controlled within the departments representing the narrow academic disciplines. These departments grow narrower and more numerous year by year as the advance of modern science results in increasing specialization. [The new] institutes and centers contrast strongly with the history of agriculture and public health [programs] in which curriculum, faculty, and research were centered in schools that were nearly autonomous.

The report is based on the authors' discussions with faculty and administrators connected with multidisciplinary programs at more than thirty universities and on their visits to six universities (unnamed in the report) deemed to have had some success in mounting such programs. "Research done under the auspices of institutes or centers is most frequently done within existing departments, and it is only the sum of research that is interdisciplinary because each individual project is divided into the disciplines and pursued independently," they said.

According to the authors, those few centers or other units found to have genuinely effective multidisciplinary programs all had two things in common—they had substantial influence or complete control over faculty hiring, promotions, and other rewards, and they enjoyed flexibility in introducing new course work and curricula and in devising degree programs. Also, in most cases the successful programs were found to have the direct support of one of the university's more senior administrators who could help provide resources and protect the programs from "traditionally minded faculty members."

The authors found that the Federal Government itself was held partly to blame for the failure of multidisciplinary programs.

A common complaint we heard at all the universities visited [they said] was that there was a general lack of funds available for such wide-ranging interdisciplinary programs. What the heads of most of these institutes found themselves doing was going through a process of genteel lying and cheating in order to get money for their programs. Oftentimes, it was necessary to emasculate the programs in order to suit the specifications for Federal funding.

All this the authors regarded as a shame, for they found great interest among both students and faculty in problem-focused environmental studies. According to the report, between ten and twenty major universities already have programs of studies of this kind far enough along to be ready for Federal funding. And, it said, more than two hundred other institutions have expressed "vigorous interest" in starting such programs and should be given planning grants. Federal support, the authors said, should provide continuing but modest "core funding" for the programs' research and education activities as a whole; "seed money" for faculty salaries and for educational innovation as programs are being started; and student aid, at levels sufficient to enable mature people who have worked professionally on environmental problems to return to the university for further studies.

According to the report, about half of the $20 million which would be needed to start or plan the new programs could come from funds already available to Federal agencies such as the departments of Interior, Transportation, HEW [Health, Education, and Welfare] and HUD [Housing and Urban Development], and the National Science Foundation [NSF]. "It is our firm opinion," the authors said, "that the Government would get more return for its money in programs of this sort than they now get from some of the existing training grants and contract research." NSF is hoping that Congress will allow it at least $6 million in fiscal 1970 for problem-focused multidisciplinary programs, some to be concerned with the environment.

The report said that there should be strong interaction between the Federal funding agencies and the universities in the development of the multidisciplinary programs—a point which DuBridge found "particularly interesting." And, in order to improve chances that the agencies would administer the grants effectively, this function should be carried out under the policy guidance of the Environmental Quality Council and of a special interagency group, the authors said.

TAXATION AS A WEAPON AGAINST POLLUTERS [7]

The power to tax is the power to destroy. But the power to tax can also be the power to preserve. And in the achievement of a more salutary environment, the same tax may be both.

Taxation is the most versatile power in the government's arsenal, and it should be used to advance the cause of an uncontaminated, uncluttered and unpolluted environment. The Federal Government's conservation agencies and the congressional committees should counsel together to develop a tax program which would maintain a clean and esthetically pleasing environment.

[7] From "Taxation Urged to Help Prevent Further Pollution," by Irston R. Barnes, reporter. Washington *Post*. p L 11. N. 9, '69. Reprinted by permission.

The tax principle involved is unimpeachable. Impose the burden on those who create the costs! Such taxes would either deter the contamination or provide the means of cleaning up the mess. The use of taxation for regulatory as well as revenue purposes has been affirmed again and again by the courts.

The root cause of most environmental pollution is a situation where some individual or company shifts some of its costs to the community. Taxation could shift the costs back to those who originate the pollution. Or if the pollution is of a particularly intractable or hazardous nature, and hence must be prevented, then prohibitory tax rates can help to attain that goal.

Any citizen with a modicum of good taste who drives through the country along any highway, or even on city streets, is offended by the litter that is a national disgrace. A recent advertisement for aluminum beer cans made the point that the company's aluminum cans would be valuable enough to be picked up and sold for scrap. Why not make them too valuable to throw on the roadside in the first place?

A Federal tax, of say, 10 cents on every soft drink bottle, beer can, liquor bottle, household plastic container, etc., that does not have a 5-cent return payment might be high enough to recycle such items back to the manufacturer for reuse. Certainly any attempt to clean such rubbish off the highways, out of streams, and off the beaches would cost at least 10 cents an item.

It is coming to be generally recognized that DDT and other highly toxic chemical pesticides are destroying life beyond our capacity to trace their evil effects. Here obviously is a place for extreme prohibitory taxes as well as a general prohibition of use in most household and agricultural applications. [See "Phasing Out DDT," in Section II, above.]

If highway billboards are offensive, as they are to most people, then a high punitive tax on all such billboards as are visible from (and hence, intrude upon) any federally aided highway would accomplish the objective without the frustrations of noncooperating state or local governments.

If the internal combustion engine is the great source of air pollution, then a steeply progressive tax on internal combustion engines based on horsepower rating and fuel consumption would encourage the use of smaller motors, and thereby supplement the use of smog-control devices.

I do not know what it would cost industry to control industrial air and water pollution, but I am sure that any realistic calculation of out-of-pocket costs imposed on residents of air-polluted communities for laundry, cleaning, painting, etc., would far outweigh any alternative costs to the pollution-creating industries.

Similarly, the costs to communities and industries in coping with polluted sources of water for household and industrial use would far outweigh the costs of control that are avoided by upstream communities and industries, the sources of pollution.

It makes more sense to use the tax power to cure the sources of environmental contamination than to collect taxes for attempted cleanups from those who have already suffered from the pollution.

Other environmental problems could usefully be solved by the tax route. Germany in the early postwar years pointed out one solution to problems of traffic congestion. The goods, traffic and freight that had been moving by highway was put back on the rails!

Is it not time to call a halt to highway building—interstate superhighways or scenic highways? Would there be any need for paving more of America if we would recognize that railway capacity is immensely more efficient than highway capacity in handling freight traffic.

A program to put freight back on the rails might mean small additions to transit times for short haul shipments, but that would be a small price to pay for highways uncluttered with trucks and an end to highway expansion. The tax power could easily change the economics of freight transport.

These examples are simply indicative of what could easily prove the most effective attack on all forms of environmental pollution and degradation. And in each instance the tax would simply recognize where community costs for environment deterioration originate.

THE COSTS OF CLEANING UP POLLUTION [8]

There has been a growing concern about pollution in the United States, and this concern has resulted in a number of pathbreaking, Federal antipollution laws during 1963-1967. Not surprisingly, Americans are indicating a new demand for the benefits of clean air and water as the available supply of these two commodities diminishes. In my judgment, however, neither legislative efforts at the national and local levels, nor the growing private clamor for new controls alter what is the central fact of pollution: it is a largely unknown, potentially disastrous phenomenon, which in spite of these recent efforts, is in many areas getting worse. And, it will continue to do so until governments, especially local governments, are put under a great deal more pressure than they currently are experiencing. What needs emphasis here is that most pollution in this country occurs in local communities not connected with interstate boundaries and thus not subject to Federal controls; therefore its elimination will finally derive from the willingness and ability of local communities to solve their own problems. . . .

I believe the solution [to our pollution problems] involves what I shall refer to as a short-run approach and long-run approach. In this context, the short-run applies to a time period during which most legal and other institutional arrangements as well as the general habits of the human participants remain essentially the same. In other words,

[8] From "Environmental Pollution and the Challenge to Traditional Economic Values," by Charles Sackrey, assistant professor of economics, Smith College. In *Man and His Environment: Catastrophe or Control?* Transcripts of lectures given at Alumnae College, May 28-30, 1969. Alumnae Association of Smith College. Northampton, Mass. '69. mimeo. p 26-43. Reprinted by permission.

short-run solutions have to do with solving social problems within the existing framework of social institutions. Alternatively, the long-run here refers to a time period extensive enough to allow changes in the organization of social institutions, and thus challenges more completely the basic values by which we live. Let me elaborate by discussing initially the short-run aspect of the problem.

If we take the word of the scientists, it is clear that one national goal should be to terminate immediately the practice of pouring filth into our environment. And, in order to do so as rapidly as possible, we must depend upon those tools already available. Initially, it is necessary to determine the costs which would be associated with a pollution abatement program to be carried out over some relatively short future period, say the five years . . . 1970-1974, which would minimize pollution in this country by the use of the best available technology.

It would be nice, indeed, if the necessary research had been done so that I could present you a complete accounting of how much it would cost Americans to finance such a program. However, these figures, like the potential dangers of pollution itself, are not known, and those available are scanty and always in the form of rough estimates. Nonetheless, I will, at the risk of being entirely wrong in some areas, provide you with some cost estimates I have uncovered.

Estimating Costs

At the outset it should be emphasized that my use of the term *cost* here refers to the estimated costs of installing the most efficient pollution abatement devices available. In other words, what I am concerned with is estimating the money costs of bringing environmental pollution in this country to an absolute minimum, given our technology and institutional habits. This concept of *pollution cost* should be distinguished from the cost we incur by tolerating pollution. This latter concept, which amounts to the money costs of living in a dirty environment, is necessarily imprecise and finally cannot be determined, since in order to calculate it one must estimate the dollar value of such inconveniences as not being able to see the sky, of dying early from emphysema, of stinking rivers, and many other similar items. I am, therefore, assuming that these inconveniences cannot be assigned a dollar value, and are too great to be tolerated in any case.

In general, my research on the costs of pollution abatement shows the estimates to be higher the more recent they are. As more evidence is accumulated, both the extent of the problem and the costs necessary to minimize it seem ever larger. In any event, I have compiled the following cost estimates for our hypothetical pollution abatement program for the 1970-1974 period. First, I have estimated that under current programs, by both government and industry, we are probably spending around $5 billion annually. Thus, during 1970-1974, if we were to continue current programs, we would spend about $25 billion. Second, I have estimated the approximate costs of the sort of five-year program which would minimize pollution, given our technology and habits. These estimates are as follows: water pollution abatement—$50 billion, most of which woud be spent on modernization of sewage treatment plants and sewer systems; air pollution control would cost about $60 billion, most of which would be spent on control of vehicular pollution; and, finally, a minimization of pollution from garbage and solid waste disposal would cost about $15 billion for the five-year period. Added together these come to a figure of $125 billion: subtract from that the $25 billion which will be spent if we continue current programs and you are left with a figure of about $100 billion more for the five-year program.

I have estimated the costs on the basis of a five-year period since I am assuming that it would take some time to install devices on cars and on factories, to build all the sewage treatment plants, etc., and generally in many ways to adjust to the somewhat different way of doing things. And, if the $100 billion costs are allocated over the same five-year period, we can derive an annual additional cost of approximately $20 billion per year. As I proceed it will become clear that the argument to follow remains essentially intact whether the annual figure is $20 billion, $25 billion or any other feasible figure. Thus, it is not crucial to my main argument whether my estimates are precise.

I should also point out here that the $100 billion in additional expenditures will be borne by households, unless for some reason tax funds already being used for military, space, and other Government programs are reallocated to pollution abatement. In the more likely event that such reallocations are not made, pollution abatement which is financed by government will be paid for by higher taxes. If industry pays the bill, they will, as a group, pass on the costs in the form of higher prices to those of us who buy their products. In short, we will pay to clean up the mess we have made, and thus, finally, we must make the decision to hire the cleaning lady.

Can We Afford It?

In a quick summary of the preceding: we need to spend about $20 billion per year beyond what we are spending now between 1970 and 1974 to minimize pollution. No question comes quicker to mind than the typically American one: can we afford it? Let me try to answer that very legitimate question.

In 1968, the gross national product of the United States was $860 billion, or about 30 per cent of everything produced in the world. Thus, the question above can be rephrased: is there any part of the $860 billion which could have been allocated for pollution abatement for the year 1968, had we initiated our five-year program in that year? Perhaps the best way to answer this is to examine what, in fact, we did do with our output in 1968, a year for which I have some interesting data.

First, some figures from the public sector—the sector which is financed by our tax payments—are revealing. Among other items we purchased through Government in 1968 were: national defense, $80.5 billion and space exploration, $4.7

billion. We also spent money through the public sector on schools, welfare, highways, the agriculture program, etc., but, for purely subjective reasons, I am going to concentrate on national defense and space exploration for a moment as a source of potential pollution abatement funds, for some interesting questions regarding them can be posed. For example: was the $30 billion spent in Vietnam in 1968 allocated to control a threat more potentially dangerous than environmental pollution? Is the excitement, romance and scientific knowledge gained from the moon program *really* as important as an environment conducive to health and esthetic pleasure? If your answer to these questions is No, that we should cut these budgets and clean up our niche, you have all of the $20 billion at hand, plus a lot left over. If, on the other hand, you agree with many Americans that the defense and space budgets are absolutely sacrosanct and delimiting them can only result in some kind of immediate foreign aggression, then we must go elsewhere to raise our funds.

We could, of course, remain in the public sector, and ask ourselves the same kinds of questions about the billions of dollars spent in 1968 to subsidize the most wealthy farmers; the billions spent on commerce, transportation and education, or expenditures in other governmental sectors. Assuming, however, that for various reasons, none of these funds could be reallocated, we are forced to abandon the public sector as a source of revenue. Don't despair, however, for what remains is the largest sector of all, the households which receive income and spend it on consumers' goods. It is instructive to investigate the nature of some of these private expenditures made in 1968.

During that year, households spent $533 billion on cars, food, clothing, recreation, education, health, and many other goods and services. What are possible ways a few billion could be reallocated from this sector into a pollution control program?

I have compiled a few figures from the consumers' sector which are interesting and relevant to answering this question. In 1968, the following approximate expenditures were made by American households for the following new products:

Electric Blenders	$100	million
Country Club Dues	200	million
Jewelry and Watches	3.5	billion
TVs, Radios, Phonographs and Records	8.0	billion
Furniture and Household Equipment ..	34.0	billion
New Autos: Foreign and Domestic	36.0	billion

(The expenditures on jewelry and watches are *sixteen times* what the Federal Government spent on water pollution control in 1968; the expenditures on country club dues are more than *twice* the Federal Government's expenditures on air pollution control during the year.)

What does all of this mean? In the way of an explanation, perhaps it would be valuable to take another look at the figures and see if there is any combination of these things which, had we done without in 1968, we could have had $20 billion available for pollution control and cleanup. Though the number of possible combinations is quite large, I have constructed my own list, and while it surely says more about my own value system than anything else, it also makes my essential point.

Let us assume, therefore, that prior to 1968, we were convinced that we could no longer afford *not* to control pollution. What could we have given up in the way of private goods alone during that year to raise the magical $20 billion?

Had we, for example, bought no new jewelry or watches, imported no diamonds, spent 10 per cent less on furniture and household appliances, purchased half as expensive or half as many radios, television sets, phonographs and records, and suffered the indignities of doing without electric blenders, and country clubs, we would have been able to allocate about $11 billion to a pollution control program. And, had each of the 10 million of us in 1968 who purchased a new automobile on average bought a $2,000 car rather than a $3,000 one, as we did, this would have amounted to a savings of $10 billion. Add these two figures and you have over $20 billion.

You should note some interesting features of this selection. First, I have not tampered with the untamperable, namely national defense. Nor have I reduced any of the other kinds of public expenditures. Note finally that even with the reallocations I have suggested, Americans would still be spending on a per capita basis more (by a large amount) for most luxury items than people in any other country. In other words, I have concentrated on luxury items in my example, thus I am not suggesting that Americans give up food, clothing, schooling, medical care, or any of the so-called necessities.

Looking at this matter from another perspective confirms the implications above that pollution abatement could be financed without serious loss to American households. Recently, GNP [gross national product] has been increasing each year by about $20 to $30 billion, even after allowance has been made for inflation. Thus, if we started a five-year abatement program in 1970 and financed it out of the difference between GNP in that year and GNP in 1969, we could still spend at least as much next year as we will spend this year on everything: consumer goods, national defense, space—the whole works. This, of course, assumes that GNP will continue to grow as much as it has in the recent past. The odds are that it will almost surely grow by enough to finance a $20 billion pollution abatement program. We are, as we have been told, an affluent society!

Are We Willing to Pay?

What I have been suggesting in several different ways is that we are ruining our environment because although we are *able,* we are not *willing,* to avoid doing so. That is the inescapable and most important conclusion of this paper. There are many reasons why this is so, but especially important are two aspects of our way of doing things. First, since pollution abatement is, like national defense, a "collective good"—that is, since no one of us can buy it separately without benefits accruing to the rest of us, we buy it together—it is not possible for any of us individually to exchange some of our consumer goods for clean air, even though we may be quite willing to do so. Unless our neighbors are equally willing to make such an exchange, it helps no one of us in any real sense to fight air pollution by selling our automobile and offering the proceeds to local tax authorities for an abatement program. Unfortunately, the only results of such an action on the part of a single individual might be that (1) he feels morally superior when he walks while everyone else drives; and (2) the local tax authority decides that he is the village idiot. Thus, a community with, for example, a severe smog problem must act collectively to solve it, in the same way it has provided other collective goods, such as police protection and public education.

The second feature of our system which allows us to spoil the environment even though we can easily afford not to, is that pollution abatement amounts to a considerable cost to many private interests, especially to certain industrial firms. An example here may help make the point. If a factory in your community is polluting a local stream, its managers, even though sympathetic to your needs, may be unable to satisfy them for the simple reason that equipment to do the job is prohibitively expensive. Especially a problem in this regard would be a factory competing with companies in other communities which do not require such equipment. In such a case, the survival of the local firm may depend upon its *not* having to install such equipment. It needs to be pointed out, however, that this kind of example does not account for a good deal of industry's hostility to pollution abatement. Frequently this hostility simply reflects a public-be-damned attitude, or reflects the judgment of the industry's management that no one should be able to tell them how to run their affairs. The recent antitrust suit brought against the auto industry, charging some firms with conspiring not to compete in the development of auto exhaust control devices, indicates that these firms may have been motivated more by stubbornness and irresponsibility than by cost considerations.

In any event, both of these characteristics of pollution abatement—the fact that abatement is a collective good and the fact that abatement programs are frequently opposed by strong private interests—go a long way toward explaining why the world's wealthiest nation has a serious pollution problem, the solution to which could be financed by only a portion of what its people spend on luxuries. . . .

The point here is that the short-run solution of environmental pollution will cost money, but the funds are more than available. What is not available in this country is the public will to (1) force politicians to reevaluate priorities at the governmental level; and/or (2) to ignore the advertisements for consumer goods and pay the taxes or higher prices probably necessary to clean up the mess the production and consumption of these goods entails. . . .

The argument above concerning causes of our inability to finance a pollution abatement program points toward potential solutions, at least in the short run. The recognition that pollution abatement is a collective good implies quite clearly that local pollution, for example, will only be solved by convincing a majority (or an important minority) in the local community that it is in their best interests not to tolerate it. The causes outlined earlier also make clear that the battles of private citizens to implement pollution abatement will, in many cases, have to be fought against well-financed opponents. In sum, those of us who want to minimize pollution must, as an initial step, convince others who use the same polluted air and water, that we will all be better off by effecting ways to clean up the environment. Showing up by yourself at the door of the local utility with a perfumed note asking them to stop ruining your children's air probably won't result in much action; showing up with a crowd of aroused neighbors is another matter entirely. Since we are, from what I can gather, not given much time to clean our nest, the immediacy of the need to start work hardly needs emphasis.

Let us assume for the sake of the rest of my argument that through some massive exertion of public will, we do in fact minimize pollution. At least, let us assume that we do everything in our power to do so. Will this solve the problem of environmental pollution deriving from human expansion? Most surely not. As I pointed out earlier, all of the previous argument relates only to the minimization of pollution in this country. I have not concerned myself as yet with the problem on an international scale, choosing to discuss only what we can do unilaterally.

It must be apparent that we are doomed if our own efforts are not combined with those of all other industrialized nations, and, in the near future, with efforts of the large populations in Asia and South America who are of necessity tearing at their own environments to get food, clothing and shelter. The prospects for air pollution of 800 million gas-powered autos in China, and another 600 million in India are awesome.

Toward a World Economy

One writer, Kenneth Boulding of Colorado University, has argued that we are rapidly moving from a "cowboy" world economy to a "spaceship" world economy. In the former, the principal motivating force behind social development is the laying to waste of the environment by producing all that can be produced as rapidly as possible. Not surprisingly, the prevailing value system in such an economy is that large output and large consumption patterns are to be esteemed and emulated. Thus, in recent history, nations with industrialized economies, with high levels of consumption and public expenditures are the envy, we keep telling ourselves, of the poor ones.

To be sure, a cowboy world economy can be pursued only for as long as new territory can be abandoned after it has been used up, and only for as long as there are significant proportions of the planet which are both fertile and uninhabited. Such characteristics no longer, unfortunately, describe our own globe. In fact, the explosion in population growth in this century is making obsolete the cowboy-economy concept much faster than most persons would have thought possible even twenty years ago. We may indeed be moving rapidly toward the era of the "spaceship world economy."

Boulding describes such an economy as one "in which the earth has become like a single spaceship, without unlimited reservoirs of anything, either for extraction or for pollution, and in which, therefore, man must find his place in a *cyclical* ecological system. . . ." In such an economy, therefore, the total output of commodities is regarded as something to be *minimized* rather than maximized, since, like the case of a spaceship filled with astronauts, all wastes must be recycled. Such an idea and its potential realization have some *large* implications for the future development of this culture as well as for all others.

One very real challenge of the spaceship concept is the threat to the one value that all of us have been trained to accept since we were born, namely, that acquiring more things makes life better. There are several variations to this theme, of course, and one cannot go a day without being reminded in the press, on the TV, in the movies and in conversation of the notion that whatever problem one has, it can be solved, or at least mitigated, by some kind of consumer product, ranging from the most direct satisfaction of an aspirin to the more indirect benefits of having luxury items of no obvious function other than ostentation. . . .

Problems deriving from the production and consumption of commodities are those of a world population of a little more than 3 billion. What can we expect the nature of the environmental pollution to be with a world population of, say 5 billion? or 10 billion? or 50 billion? It is clear, at least to me, that modern man cannot for much longer pursue his affairs either here or abroad without substantially changing his notion that happiness is a simple function of material acquisitions.

In this country, where the total output available has been for some time considerably greater than that necessary to provide everyone with basic necessities, it has been only very recently that some among us are beginning to question the merits of this kind of life-style. Is there, therefore, any reason to believe that poor countries, with most of the world's populations, will stop their own "growth-mania" at the point when they are fed, clothed and housed adequately? Surely, we are able to provide a more instructive example to the rest of the world about how to solve the problems of an advanced industrial nation than the simple one of allowing our environment to degenerate through sheer negligence.

As must be apparent, I take quite seriously the possibility that we are moving toward the development of something akin to Boulding's "spaceship world economy," and I believe that—in the not-too-distant future—it is going to be necessary for man to call into question a set of values about what constitutes the good life which has been dominant in recent history. Perhaps it is time to determine as objectively as possible whether in fact our new automobiles are worth giving up clean air for; whether our new trinkets are really worth the industrial pollution caused by their production and the blight caused when we tire of them and toss them to the side; whether putting a man on the moon is really as important as research to determine the exact state of our environment and how we can make it healthier; whether, finally, we will take the lead among nations in indicating our superiority over other animals by logically and rationally pursuing a future which will perpetuate our species.

So much for my main argument. I have offered a point of view which I hope will induce you to question your own judgment and which will act as the basis of a dialogue between yourselves and others concerning one of the more serious aspects of man's relationship to his environment. We are not, after all, like a defenseless pillbug, crawling across a sidewalk while children are playing hop-scotch, waiting to be crushed by a foot gone astray. We are human beings with enormous talent for solving problems, and therefore are quite able, first, to clean up our contemporary ecological niche, and second, to make plans for a future consistent with the welfare of generations to come. In any case, whatever problem environmental pollution represents today, by tomorrow, when there will be more people, concentrated in larger metropolitan areas, producing more output, it will be worse. Thus, each day we allow to pass without making a determined effort to clean up our nest implies an enormous cost, both to ourselves and to those who, hopefully, will follow us.

CAN THE COURTS HELP? [9]

"For a long time I made speeches. I thought that was the answer. Now I am convinced the answer is in the courtroom." So spoke Dr. Clarence C. Gordon, botany professor at the University of Montana to more than one thousand lawyers at the recent Denver, Colorado, convention of the American Trial Lawyers Association.

"The nation just hasn't time to wait to correct environmental insults," he warned—a warning echoed by noted conservationist, Dr. Charles F. Wurster, Jr., of the State University of New York, Attorney Victor J. Yannacone, Jr., of the Environmental Defense Fund, consumer crusader Ralph Nader and Professor James W. Jeans of the University of Missouri-Kansas Law School.

The lawyers were hearing for the first time why they must join the front ranks of fighters to preserve our biosphere from disintegrating.

They were being told—in no uncertain terms—that "insults to our environment by modern technology" belonged in a new category of "corporate crime."

[9] From "Can Law Reclaim Man's Environment?" by Richard S. Jacobson, editor of *Trial*, national legal news magazine. *Trial*. 5:10-11. Ag.-S. '69. Reprinted by permission.

Nader urged them to treat this crime as "one which utterly dwarfs into insignificance crime on the streets—in terms of people injured and killed because of dangerous machinery, pollution, and unsafe household products.

"And a major group of corporate criminals are those industries responsible for environmental pollution," he said.

"Those companies are pushing mankind to the brink of environmental doomsday," Dr. Gordon added.

Yannacone—who through the Environmental Defense Fund has been battling U.S. and state governmental agencies, large industries and the many self-motivated groups— declared that civil law suits, based on damages, are "necessary to protect Americans fast enough before they are dead."

Every member of the trial bar [he said] must knock at the door of courthouses throughout the nation and seek the protection of equity for our environment.

Let each man and every corporation so use his property as not to injure that of another, particularly so as not to injure that which is common property of all the people. Let no wrong be without a remedy.

Yannacone made these points: that legislative relief is too slow and cumbersome; that United States agencies (the Army Corps of Engineers, Department of Agriculture, Atomic Energy Commission), state flood control agencies, etc. are too self-centered in their role as defendant, judge and jury; that the billion-dollar agriculture industry sways state legislatures even in the face of death-dealing pesticides (DDT and other chlorinated hydrocarbonates); and that modern scientific methods have been developed to determine relative social costs and benefits of "public improvement" projects for this and coming generations.

Yannacone said:

Conventional conservation education and action will not save any natural resource which has become the object of private greed or public blundering.

Only imaginative legal action on behalf of the general public in class actions for declaratory judgments and injunctive relief will get the story told and lay the matter before the conscience of the community in a forum where the conflict can be resolved and evidence tested in cross-examination.

Although we in the trial bar consider it a major part of our professional obligation to avoid litigation, and encourage settlement and compromise, there is a time not to settle. There is a time not to compromise. There is a time to try the case. Litigation seems the only rational way to focus the attention of our legislators on the basic problems of human existence—the protection of the basic elements of our environment, air and water and the diverse, viable populations of plants and animals on the ground, in the air and in the seas.

Do we have sufficient time on this earth to delay taking action—legislative and judicial? *Trial* has made an exhaustive survey of environmental insults and ensuing dangers, and it states editorially: We don't have time.

As Barry Commoner, editor of the Center for Biology of Natural Systems, Washington University, St. Louis, Missouri, warned the Senate Governmental Relations Subcommittee:

> We need to reassess our attitudes toward the natural world on which our technology intrudes. . . . Modern technology has so stressed the web of process in the living environment at its most vulnerable points that there is little leeway left in the system.
> And the time is short; we must begin now to learn how to make our technological power conform to the more powerful constraints of the living environment.

ESTABLISHMENT OF COUNCIL OF ENVIRONMENTAL ADVISERS [10]

It is particularly fitting that my first official act in this new decade is to approve the National Environmental Policy Act.

The past year [1969] has seen the creation of a President's Cabinet Committee on Environmental Quality, and we have devoted many hours to the pressing problems of pollution control, airport location, wilderness preservation, highway construction and population trends.

[10] President Nixon's statement on environmental pollution, January 1, 1970. Text from Associated Press dispatch as printed in the New York *Times.* Ja. 2, '70. p 12.

By my participation in these efforts I have become further convinced that the 1970s absolutely must be the years when America pays its debt to the past by reclaiming the purity of its air, its waters and our living environment. It is literally now or never.

I, therefore, commend the Congress and particularly the sponsors of this bill, Senator [Ted] Stevens [Republican, Alaska] and [Henry M.] Jackson [Democrat, Washington] and Representative [John W.] Dingell [Democrat, Michigan] for this clear legislative policy declaration. Under the provisions of this law a three-member Council of Environmental Advisers will be appointed.

I anticipate that they will occupy the same close advisory relation to the President that the Council of Economic Advisers does in fiscal and monetary matters. The environmental advisers will be assisted by a compact staff in keeping me thoroughly posted on current problems and advising me on how the Federal Government can act to solve them.

Opposes Second Group

In the near future I will forward to the Senate names of highly qualified individuals to help both the Cabinet and me in the critical decisions that will affect the quality of life in the United States for years to come. I will then take the necessary executive action to reconstitute the Cabinet committee and its staff to avoid duplication of function.

On the latter point, I know that the Congress has before it a proposal to establish yet another staff organization to deal with environmental problems in the Executive Office of the President. I believe this would be a mistake.

No matter how pressing the problem, to overorganize, to overstaff or to compound the levels of review and advice seldom brings earlier or better results.

We are most interested in results. The act I have signed gives us an adequate organization and a good statement of direction. We are determined that the decade of the seventies will be known as the time when this country regained a productive harmony between man and nature.

SWEDEN'S ANTIPOLLUTION PROGRAM [11]

Larger than California, but with a population of only 8 million, Sweden is far from being plagued by the pollution problems that afflict most industrialized nations. But the Swedes have not remained altogether unscathed, nor are they unmindful of the environmental ruin now found in places that once could follow the maxim that "the answer to pollution is dilution." As a consequence, Sweden has undertaken an ambitious and relatively expensive effort to clean up whatever mess now exists and to prevent further ones from developing. Not surprisingly, Sweden was the first nation to impose a total ban on the use of DDT, aldrin, dieldrin, and other chlorinated hydrocarbons, effective the beginning of ... [1970]. As one official explained, "It wasn't very difficult to do. Very little if any of these are manufactured here, and besides, we made the farmers realize that they are the first to suffer from exposure."

In many respects, the Swedish approach to the problem is similar to the approach in other countries: research, the establishment of standards, and the provision of matching government grants to help industry and local communities buy antipollution equipment. But the Swedish effort also contains several special elements that are intriguing when viewed against the so-far doleful U.S. experience in dealing with pollution. First of all, though fairly strict legislation is on the books—as is the case in the United States—the Swedish government, recognizing the link between law enforcement and public opinion, has undertaken a sizable adult education program aimed at creating in each community a corps of well-informed citizens who can organize public hearings

[11] From "Pollution Control: Sweden Sets Up an Ambitious New Program," by Daniel S. Greenberg, foreign editor of *Science*. *Science*. 166:200-1. O. 10, '69. Copyright 1969 by the American Association for the Advancement of Science. Reprinted by permission.

and confront industrial and civic officials on what they are doing about pollution. . . .

[During 1969] under the auspices of the Ministry of Education, some 250,000 persons received at least a few evenings' instruction on the technical and legal aspects of pollution. From this number, about 10,000 accepted the offer of an additional two weeks' instruction, and, from this second group, about 1,000 throughout the country were picked to conduct public inquiries and, in general, agitate in behalf of pollution control. The program is just getting out of the classroom stage, and its effectiveness remains to be demonstrated. But one of the country's most diligent antipollution crusaders, a young physician and researcher, Hans Palmstierna, who is secretary of the government's central coordinating board in the pollution field, is quite optimistic.

With the new laws that we have, and the public getting more and more aroused [he said], we have every reason to make progress. . . . It's down to the level now where people who never thought about this problem before are feeling angry about their fishing and other recreation places being ruined. And now they know they don't have to feel helpless about it. There's something that can be done.

Within the government, the operating agency for dealing with pollution is the National Nature Conservancy Office, which is possibly unique among such national organizations in that it exists as a branch of the Ministry of Agriculture. This placement was largely accidental, having grown out of the Ministry's concern over fish poisonings from mercury compounds used as fungicides in Sweden's huge pulp and paper industry. In 1965, after it became clear that the mercury did not decompose but simply continued to accumulate, restrictions were imposed, and the beginning of this year brought an end to the use of mercury compounds. But in the meantime the Ministry of Agriculture had become increasingly involved with the pollution issue, and finally, in 1967, its interest culminated in the creation of the Conservancy Office, which has a current staff of about 175 and annual funds, controlled directly or shared with other organizations, of about $50 million.

Benefits of Structure

Though the Conservancy's position as a branch of the Ministry of Agriculture was the result more of chance than of design, it is said to offer several important benefits. As an official explained it, agriculture is in a relative state of decline in the Swedish economy and now employs only about 10 per cent of the labor force. Interest in pollution control, on the other hand, is on the way up, and so are expenditures. "In this situation," he said, "the Ministry is delighted to have a new and expanding responsibility." Serving as the national policy-making body for antipollution activity is the Consulting Board for Environmental Problems, whose twenty-four members include ten scientists, plus representatives of labor, industry, finance, and the press. Communities and regions have authority to deal with their pollution problems. But the guiding force is the Conservancy Office, with its branches for nature conservation, water and air, and research.

And the guiding principles are to be found in fairly stringent legislation that went into effect . . . [in July 1969]. Titled the Environmental Protection Act, the new law contains provisions for the use of money to work against existing sources of pollution, and for the use of authority to prevent new pollution. Thus, under the Act, an experimental fund of about $50 million, to be spent over a five-year period, has been created to pay 25 per cent of the cost for providing antipollution equipment for established industries. (Some Swedish conservationists complain that this undercuts the principle of the polluter paying for abatement, but otherwise they seem to be quite pleased with the Act.) For industrial plants yet to be built, the Act requires that permission first be obtained from a specially created body, the Concessions Board for the Protection of the Environment, a four-member group with authority to set limits on how much pollutant may be put out into the environment. The Board consists of a chairman trained in the law, a technical specialist in the area of pollution, and two persons without any particular affiliation. Because of its newness, the Board has yet to reveal any pattern of operations, but since one of the members will be drawn from the Nature Conservancy Office, a stronghold of antipollution fervor, it is unlikely that the Board will become a tool of evasion, as has been the case with similar organizations in the United States.

Though the Baltic Sea is severely polluted from sources within Sweden as well as from other countries, and since the mercury problem had reached serious proportions before the total ban went into effect, the striking thing about the Swedish antipollution effort is that, by and large, it reflects foresight rather than emergency response to an intolerable situation. Thus, in a paper that the Nature Conservancy prepared for presentation at the European Conference on Nature Conservation, to be held in Strasbourg . . . February [1970], it is noted that, in major Swedish cities, "The content of sulfur dioxide is less than in the most polluted regions in the U.S.A., England, and Germany by a factor of two, and the values for soot are five to ten times less than corresponding English values." Nevertheless, under the new law, the Swedes have limited the sulfur content of fuel oil to 2.5 per cent by weight, and municipalities are free to set even lower limits. . . . [In 1970] progressively more severe limitations will go into effect on pollution from automotive vehicles, starting with a limit of 0.7 gram per liter for lead content in motor fuel. Though few, if any, of Sweden's inland waterways have reached the stage of being too thick to navigate and too thin to cultivate, it is planned to have sewage purification plants serving all built-up areas within a few years. Communities will be eligible for grants of 30 to 50 per cent to meet the cost, and backing up this assistance is the new law, which states that municipal waste may not be discharged without a permit.

Industrial Concentration a Boon

Industrial trends are also expected to provide an important boost for Sweden's antipollution program. Though pulp- and paper-making are on the increase, production in these fields is being concentrated in fewer, larger plants; this makes it a simpler matter to treat and to police the handling of effluents. There is also a trend toward centralized community-heating plants. This arises mainly from economic considerations, but it also makes it easier to cut down on pollutants. With hydroelectric sources fairly well exploited by now, Sweden is planning a major move into atomic energy, with the expectation that possibly as many as fifteen large power plants may be built in the south and central parts of the country before the end of the century. But, if the Nature Conservancy has its way, these plants will be sited in conformity with a comprehensive master plan designed to minimize their ecological effects. And, thereby, a high value will be placed on what is referred to as "the social aspect" of conservation. As the Nature Conservancy states in its presentation to the forthcoming Strasbourg conference, the pleasure that people derive from the countryside merits just as much attention as anything else in planning a clean environment. Though the Swedes probably excel in foresight, will, and resources for dealing with pollution, there are aspects of the problem that go beyond their reach. It is estimated that from 15 to 50 per cent of the sulfur dioxide in their atmosphere originates in other countries; some of it, it is believed, comes from Britain, which has been looking after its own problems by introducing taller smokestacks so as to get the stuff carried off by winds. The Baltic Sea is in sad shape, but none of its major polluters show as much fervor as the Swedes for getting things cleaned up. To the extent that matters are within their own control, the Swedes apparently possess an unmatched determination to avoid the damage that other nations have inflicted upon themselves. The effort is just beginning, but it could be an inspiring one.

UNITED NATIONS EFFORTS TO PROTECT
OUR ENVIRONMENT [12]

The deterioration of the human environment through the population explosion, pollution of air and water, and other disruptions of the ecological balance has rapidly come to the fore as a major international problem, which menaces the quality and ultimately the survival of human life on the entire planet. In the United Nations the urgency of considering the total effect on the human environment of technological progress and industrialization—the major causes of pollution—was first stressed by Sweden in a memorandum put before ECOSOC [United Nations Economic and Social Council] in the summer of 1968.

The Council responded by unanimously recommending that the General Assembly focus attention on the importance of environmental problems by means of an international conference. On the basis of a Swedish proposal, the twenty-third Assembly decided to convene such a conference in 1972 to alert governments (and world public opinion) to the dangers involved in the changing relations between man and his environment, and to their responsibilities for taking both preventive and corrective action. The Assembly further requested the Secretary-General, in consultation with the Advisory Committee on the Application of Science and Technology to Development, to report through ECOSOC to the twenty-fourth Assembly on the nature, scope, and progress of work on the human environment and on the main problems facing both developed and developing countries in this field.

As the Swedish representative explained to the Assembly, man's survival depends on an infinitely complex system of relationships and balances among countless living organisms, existing in or on the extremely thin crust of the earth, or just above it. "The system has a remarkable capacity for adaptation and regeneration; but nature's patience has a limit."

[12] From "Issues Before the 24th General Assembly: Science and Technology—Human Environment." *International Conciliation*. no 574:52-7. S. '69.

Although modern technology is indispensable for economic
and social progress, it can set off a reaction with "unforeseen
harmful effects," and many of these effects cannot be undone.
"Even if we avoid the risk of blowing up the planet," he
warned, "we may, by changing its face, unwittingly be parties
to a process with the same fatal outcome."

The Secretary-General Reports

The Secretary-General's report on problems of the human environment sounds a similar ominous note: "If current
trends continue, the future of life on earth could be endangered." Thus it is urgent "to focus world attention on those
problems which threaten humanity in an environment that
permits the realization of the highest human aspirations."
The report seeks to unravel some of the complexities of environmental deterioration and to identify causes and types
of problems as a first step in setting forth areas for action.
Three underlying causes of the environmental crisis are
cited: accelerated population growth, increased urbanization, and new and expanded technology—all associated with
increased demands for space, food, and natural resources.

In less than four centuries, the human population has
grown from an estimated half billion persons to seven times
that number and is expected to double in the next fifty years.
At present, "all areas of the earth's surface have been to some
degree modified by man." Nearly 1.25 billion acres of arable
land have already been lost through erosion and salinization.
Two thirds of the world's forests have been rendered unproductive. An estimated 150 types of birds and animals have
become extinct due to human actions, and over a thousand
other types are endangered.

The rate of urbanization is greatest in the developing
countries. In the period from 1920 to the year 2000, their
urban population will have grown twentyfold from 100 million to 2,000 million. In the same period developed countries
will have undergone a fourfold increase in urbanization.
This process is condemning millions of people to life in over-

crowded slums with their problems of noise, disease, crime, and lack of educational and recreational facilities. As noted in the Secretary-General's report, urbanization is not in itself damaging to the environment. With proper planning and control and at a slower rate, urbanization "should enhance and not detract from environmental quality," since it can relieve pressure on rural areas and provide better and more diverse goods and services as well as attractive habitats. However, governments, particularly in the developing countries, have not prepared for urbanization; for example, in these countries disease in the cities is increasing despite advances in medicine.

Advanced industrialization, again, need not be harmful, and in fact it is of vital importance to nations seeking to improve their living standards. Here, too, lack of concern and planning has had serious consequences. Industrial waste—in recent times atomic waste, smoke from combustion of fossil fuels, and exhaust from automobiles—has created major health hazards. Fresh- and saltwater bodies are being contaminated by wastes, resulting in the poisoning of fish and loss of recreational facilities. Two recent events have brought home with shocking impact the dimensions of this aspect of pollution. One is the widespread, possibly permanent damage to the beaches of Santa Barbara, California, by oil leaking from an offshore well. Another is the catastrophic poisoning of the Rhine—already known as the sewer of Europe —probably by an insecticide, which caused the death of some 40 million fish.

Indiscriminate use of insecticides, fertilizers, and hard detergents is causing untold havoc to animals and vegetation all over the world. The pesticide DDT provides a good example of the complex demands that must be met to safeguard the human environment. It is believed that minute amounts of the chemical can reduce by as much as 75 per cent photosynthesis in marine plants—the process which creates the oxygen in the earth's atmosphere. Critics of DDT claim that it is no longer an essential pesticide, since many

harmful insects have developed immunity to it and other
less destructive pesticides are now available to take its place.
(Denmark and Sweden are the only countries that have taken
steps to prohibit the use of the chemical on a national scale,
and two states in the United States—Arizona and Michigan—
have also banned its use.) DDT, however, has its defenders,
notably the Director-General of the World Health Organization, M. G. Candau, who has counseled against restrictions
on the pesticide in countries where the eradication of insect-
borne diseases is important. The concept of malaria eradication, he said, rests "completely" on the continued use of
DDT, which also has the advantage of being very
inexpensive.

National, Regional and World Needs

The Secretary-General's report classifies environmental
problems on three levels according to their geographic extent
and to the types of national and international action needed
to deal with them: (1) human settlement problems affecting
local areas and requiring action mainly by local and national
authorities, such as rapid urbanization and the decline of
rural settlements; (2) territorial problems of land areas and
nonoceanic and coastal waters, which must be safeguarded
by governmental action and regional arrangements; and (3)
global problems affecting all countries and requiring international agreement and joint action. Some hazards, such as
pollution, are found at all three levels, and one task is to
determine where the most effective action can be taken. Thus
in the case of water pollution, urban sewage plants require
cooperation between city and national agencies; conservation schemes for major river basins demand regional action,
as in the Mekong, La Plata, or the Rhine rivers; and prevention of oceanic pollution requires international agreement.

The report found that present efforts to meet environmental problems are being carried out on a fragmentary
basis by traditional agencies, even though for some time
there has been an urgent need for an integrated approach at

the national level and an overall view at the international level. It pointed out that preventive action to protect the environment is seldom taken into account when carrying out development plans, that the considerable amount of scientific and technical knowledge available to deal with environmental problems is not being used sufficiently, and that there is a need for further research on global physical and biological phenomena, sociocultural factors, nonpollution techniques, and rational and conservative use of resources. The report concluded that a major area for international action will be in worldwide or regional legislation, standardization, and conventions dealing with these problems.

In making suggestions for the United Nations Conference on the Human Environment, the report underscored the pressing need for new attitudes and for exchange of experience on the concrete problem of action by public authorities to plan, manage, and control the environment. The Conference, it emphasized, should not be another forum for technical discussion but should define administrative and legislative solutions. It is essential to realize that environmental problems are global, affecting both developed and developing countries. "No nation can any longer be isolated from these global pressures. . . . We all live in one biosphere within which space and resources, though vast, are limited." In addition, policies of environmental preservation must be viewed as part of the long-term and sustained development of resources for economic and social progress, and not as a restriction upon progress.

A number of practical suggestions were made regarding the Conference, in particular the creation of a fund to ensure that representatives from the poorer countries will be able to attend. It was proposed, moreover, that the Conference set up four substantive commissions to deal with human settlement and industrial development, rational use and development of natural resources, environmental pollution, and maintenance of the values of the human environment. It was also suggested that four "strategic" commissions

should be established to deal with environmental aspects of
economic and social planning, financial policies, public administration and legislation, and regional and international
cooperation.

BIBLIOGRAPHY

An asterisk (*) preceding a reference indicates that the article or a part of it has been reprinted in this book.

BOOKS, PAMPHLETS, AND DOCUMENTS

*Alumnae Association of Smith College. Man and his environment: catastrophe or control? transcripts of the lectures given at Alumnae College, May 28-30, 1969. The Association. Northampton, Mass. '69. mimeo.
    Reprinted in this volume: Environmental pollution and the challenge to traditional economic values. Charles Sackrey. p 26-43.

American Chemical Society. Cleaning our environment—the chemical basis for action. The Society. 1155 16th St. N.W. Washington, D.C. 20036. '69.
    Review article: Science. 165:1104-7. S. 12, '69. The environment: ACS report is practical anti-pollution guide. P. M. Boffey.

Briggs, Peter. Water; the vital essence. Harper. '67.

Carr, D. E. The breath of life. Norton. '65.

Carson, Rachel. The sea around us. Oxford University Press. '51.

Carson, Rachel. Silent spring. Houghton. '62.

Ciriacy-Wantrup, Siegfried von and Parsons, J. J. eds. Natural resources: quality and quantity. University of California Press. '67.

Commoner, Barry. Science and survival. Viking. '66.

Darling, F. F. and Milton, J. P. eds. Future environments of North America. Natural History Press. '66.

Dasmann, R. F. A different kind of country. Macmillan. '68.

Dasmann, R. F. Environmental conservation. 2d ed. Wiley. '68.

Dubos, R. J. So human an animal. Scribner. '68.

Edberg, Rolf. On the shred of a cloud; tr. by Sven Ahman. University of Alabama Press. '69.

Elder, Frederick. Crisis in Eden: a religious study of man and environment. Abingdon. '70.

Ewald, W. R. Jr. ed. Environment and change; the next 50 years. Indiana University Press. '68.

Ewald, W. R. Jr. ed. Environment and policy: the next 50 years. Indiana University Press. '68.

211

Fisher, James and others. Wildlife in danger. Viking. '69.

Goldman, M. I. ed. Controlling pollution; the economics of a cleaner America. Prentice-Hall. '67.

Grava, Sigurd. Urban planning aspects of water pollution control. Columbia University Press. '69.

Grossman, M. L. and others. Our vanishing wilderness. Grosset. '69.

Hay, John. In defense of nature. Little. '69.

Herfindahl, O. C. and Kneese, A. V. Quality of the environment; an economic approach to some problems in using land, water and air. Johns Hopkins Press (for Resources for the Future). '65.

Hoult, D. P. ed. Oil on the sea. Plenum Press. '69.

Krutch, J. W. Great chain of life. Houghton. '57.

Leinwand, Gerald and Popkin, Gerald. Air and water pollution. Washington Square Press. '69.

McCarthy, R. D. The ultimate folly; war by pestilence, asphyxiation and defoliation. Knopf. '69.

*McCoy, C. B. Toward a policy on pollution; remarks to Executives' Conference on Water Pollution Abatement, United States Department of the Interior, Washington, D.C., October 24, 1969. The Author. E. I. du Pont de Nemours & Company, Inc. Wilmington, Del. 19898.

McHarg, I. L. Design with nature. Natural History Press. '69.

Marine, Gene. America the raped. Simon & Schuster. '69.

Marx, Wesley. The frail ocean. Coward. '67.

Moss, F. E. The water crisis. Praeger. '67.

Murphy, E. F. Governing nature. Quadrangle. '67.

Nash, Roderick. Wilderness and the American mind. Yale University Press. '67.

National Academy of Sciences. Committee on Resources and Man. Resources & man: a study & recommendations. Freeman. '69.

National Research Council. Division of Biology and Agriculture. Eutrophication: causes, consequences, correctives. National Academy of Sciences. 2101 Constitution Ave. N.W. Washington, D.C. 20418. '69.

Nikolaieff, G. A. ed. The water crisis. (Reference Shelf. v 38, no 6) Wilson. '67.

Osborn, Fairfield. Our plundered planet. Little. '68.

Perloff, H. S. ed. The quality of the urban environment; essays on new resources in an urban age. Johns Hopkins Press (for Resources for the Future). '69.

Ridker, R. G. The economic costs of air pollution. Praeger. '67.

Rienow, Robert and Rienow, L. T. Moment in the sun; a report on the deteriorating quality of the American environment. Dial. '67.

Shepard, Paul and McKinley, Daniel, eds. The subversive science; essays toward an ecology of man. Houghton. '69.

Smith, F. E. The politics of conservation. Pantheon. '66.

Smithsonian Institution. The fitness of man's environment. The Smithsonian Institution Press. '68.

Stewart, G. R. Not so rich as you think. Houghton. '68.

United States. Congress. House of Representatives. Sciences and Astronautics Committee. Technology, processes of assessment and choices, report of National Academy of Sciences. 90th Congress, 2d session. Supt. of Docs. Washington, D.C. 20402. '69.

*United States. Department of Health, Education, and Welfare. Public Health Service. The consumer protection and environmental health service. (Publication no 1872) The Service. Washington, D.C. 20201. '68.

> *Reprinted in this volume*: The consumer protection and environmental health service. C. C. Johnson, Jr. p 1-4. Food and drug administration. H. L. Ley, Jr. p 5-7; National air pollution control administration. J. T. Middleton. p 8-9; Environmental control administration. C. A. Hansen. p 10-12.

United States. Department of Health, Education, and Welfare. Task Force on Environmental Health and Related Problems. Strategy for livable environment. Supt. of Docs. Washington, D.C. 20402. '67.

United States. Department of the Interior. Man—an endangered species? Supt. of Docs. Washington, D.C. 20402. '68.

United States. President's Council on Recreation and Natural Beauty. From sea to shining sea; a report on the American environment—our natural heritage. Supt. of Docs. Washington, D.C. 20402. '68.

Whyte, W. H. Jr. The last landscape. Doubleday. '68.

Wood, F. E. and Wood, F. D. Animals in danger; the story of vanishing American wildlife. Dodd. '68.

PERIODICALS

*America. 120:580-2. My. 17, '69. Air pollution. Daniel Briehl.

Aviation Week & Space Technology. 91:35. N. 17, '69. New aircraft noise requirements detailed.

*Bulletin of the Atomic Scientists. 25:37. Ap. '69. Antipollution technology: the electric car; excerpt from address. B. C. Netschert.

*Bulletin of the Atomic Scientists. 25:8-10. My. '69. Outwitting the patient assassin: the human use of lake pollution. H. B. Gotaas.

*Bulletin of the Atomic Scientists. 25:11-16. My. '69. Environmental noise pollution: a new threat to sanity. D. F. Anthrop.

Bulletin of the Atomic Scientists. 25:47-8+. My. '69. Conservation for conservation's sake? Eugene Rabinowitch.

*Bulletin of the Atomic Scientists. 25:35-7. O. '69. Cars and air pollution. Laura Fermi.

Bulletin of the Atomic Scientists. 25:11-14. D. '69. Arrogance toward the landscape: a problem in water planning. R. L. Nace.

Centennial Review. 13:123-37. Spring '69. An ecologist looks at his environment. J. E. Cantlon.

*Center Magazine. 2:7-12. My. '69. Polluting the environment. Lord Ritchie-Calder.

*Christian Science Monitor. p 7. O. 23, '69. Project seeks to eliminate all waste. Neal Stanford.

Christian Science Monitor. p 1+. N. 1, '69. The insidious nature of chemical pollution. R. C. Cowen.

Christian Science Monitor. p 3. N. 13, '69. Countdown on DDT. R. C. Cowen.

Cornell Law Review. 55:113-28. N. '69. Continental shelf oil disasters: challenge to international pollution control. D. M. O'Connell.

Environment. 11:2-13+. Jl.-Ag. '69. Underground nuclear testing.

Environment. 11:14-33. Jl.-Ag. '69. Earth, air, water. Justin Frost.

*Environment. 11:2-16. N. '69. The black tide. Julian McCaull.

Environment. 11:17-23. N. '69. No deposit, no return. R. R. Grinstead.

Esquire. 72:8+. N. '69. The challenge of the seventies. Arthur Godfrey.

Futurist. 3:34-5. Ap. '69. Is man's industry upsetting world weather? J. M. Mitchell.

Impact of Science on Society (UNESCO) 19:103-216. Ap.-Je. '69.
Entire issue devoted to environmental problems.

*International Conciliation. no 574:52-7. S. '69. Issues before the 24th General Assembly: science and technology—human environment.

Life. 67:60A-61. Jl. 4, '69. Letter from Lindbergh. C. A. Lindbergh.

*Life. 67:32. Ag. 1, '69. Editorial [threatened America].

*Life. 67:33-43. Ag. 1, '69. Threatened America. Donald Jackson.

*Look. 33:44-50+. S. 9, '69. The assault on the Everglades. Anthony Wolff.

*Look. 33:25-7. N. 4, '69. America the beautiful? David Perlman.

Nation. 208:795-6. Je. 23, '69. Lake Superior, private dump. Gladwin Hill.

Nation. 209:134-7. Ag. 25, '69. Poisons, profits and politics. Ruth Harmer.

Nation. 209:632-5. D. 8, '69. Pollution goes underground. D. M. Evans.

Nation. 209:729-32. D. 29, '69. Vandal ideology. Scott Paradise.

*National Observer. p 18+. Ag. 18, '69. Struggling to control growing trash heaps. E. A. Roberts, Jr.

New Republic. 161:10-11. D. 13, '69. Raiding the forests. Michael McCloskey.

*New Scientist. 44:66-7. O. 9, '69. How air pollution alters weather. Eric Aynsley.

New York Times. p 26. Ap. 28, '69. Technology and environment: senators hear gloomy appraisal. R. H. Phelps.

New York Times. p 31. Ap. 30, '69. Experts foresee noisier world with little being done about it. Gladwin Hill.

New York Times. p 47. My. 14, '69. Ore waste topic at lake hearing. Gladwin Hill.

New York Times. p 16. Je. 2, '69. Hole in pollution law. Gladwin Hill.

New York Times. p 1+. Je. 16, '69. Major U.S. cities face emergency in trash disposal; growing national problems may parallel the crisis in air and water pollution. Gladwin Hill.

New York Times. p E 16. Je. 22, '69. The world is running out of raw materials. Walter Sullivan.

New York Times. p 21. Je. 25, '69. Northwest told daring action is needed to avert "environmental disaster." L. E. Davies.

New York Times. p 1+. Ag. 27, '69. Nixon to spur competition to produce low-pollution vehicle for 1990's. Neil Sheehan.

New York Times. p 7. Ag. 28, '69. U.S. is criticized on environment. Gladwin Hill.

New York Times. p 28. Ag. 31, '69. Technology peril stirs scientists. Cleve Mathews.

*New York Times. p 1+. O. 19, '69. Air pollution grows despite rising public alarm. Gladwin Hill.

New York Times. p 44. O. 20, '69. Man—the most endangered species. Robert Bendiner.

*New York Times. p 44. N. 14, '69. Phasing out DDT.

New York Times. p 39+. N. 15, '69. Environmental suits crowd courts. Israel Shenker.

New York Times. p 1+. N. 21, '69. Partial DDT ban starts in 30 days, virtual halt by '71. R. D. Lyons.

New York Times. p 28. D. 29, '69. Crisis of the environment. A. L. Huxtable.

New York Times. p 14. D. 30, '69. Strict ban on DDT is sought in suits. H. M. Schmeck, Jr.

New York Times. p 26. D. 30, '69. Students eager for role as advisers on pollution. J. H. Fenton.

*New York Times. p 1+; 12. Ja. 2, '70. Nixon promises an urgent fight to end pollution; with text of Nixon statement.

New York Times. p 7. Ja. 22, '70. Nuclear disposal of waste studied; scientists predict re-use of converted refuse. J. N. Wilford.

New York Times. p 1+. Ja. 23, '70. Nixon stressing quality of life asks in State of Union message for battle to save environment. R. B. Semple, Jr.

New York Times. p 1+. Ja. 23, '70. $10-billion asked for clean water. E. W. Kenworthy.

New York Times. p 74. Ja. 29, '70. State is suing to hasten control of jet pollution. Richard Witkin.

New York Times. p 22+. Ja. 30, '70. Nixon appoints 3 in pollution war. R. B. Semple, Jr.

New York Times Magazine. p 24-5+. Ja. 14, '68. Jet noise is getting awful. R. G. Sherrill.

New York Times Magazine. p 87+. My. 4, '69. Only the giant car-eater can save us. D. E. Carr.

New York Times Magazine. p 32-3+. O. 5, '69. Saving the world the ecologist's way. R. W. Stock.

New York Times Magazine. p 32-3+. O. 12, '69. Santa Barbarans cite an 11th commandment: thou shalt not abuse the earth. Ross Macdonald and Robert Easton.

New York Times Magazine. p 46-7+. N. 23, '69. Noise is a slow agent of death. Anthony Bailey.

New Yorker. 44:51-2. Ap. 13, '68. Reporter at large: the ambient air. Edith Iglauer.

Newsweek. 75:30-47+. Ja. 26, '70. The ravaged environment.

Oceans. 1:52-7. Je. '69. Developing environmental awareness: a new approach to an old problem. R. B. Linsky.

Population Bulletin. 24:1-24. D. '68. The thin slice of life.

*Progressive. 33:13-18. N. '69. Our polluted planet. G. A. Nelson.

*Reader's Digest. 94:179-81+. F. '69. America the (formerly) beautiful. J. N. Miller.

Reader's Digest. 94:106-10. Mr. '69. Battle of San Francisco Bay. Earl Selby.

*Reader's Digest. 94:213+. My. '69. The great American river cleanup. Wolfgang Langewiesche.

Saturday Review. 52:18-21. My. 10, '69. Finding lemonade in Santa Barbara's oil. Garrett Hardin.

*Saturday Review. 52:19-21+. S. 20, '69. Life on a dying lake. Peter Schrag.

Saturday Review. 52:81-6. D. 6, '69. Green light for the smogless car. John Lear.

*Science. 165:44-6. Jl. 4, '69. Environmental quality: Nixon's new [Environment Quality] Council raises doubts. L. J. Carter.

Science. 165:572-3+. Ag. 8, '69. Water-pollution control: trouble at headquarters. L. J. Carter.

*Science. 166:200-1. O. 10, '69. Pollution control: Sweden sets up an ambitious new program. D. S. Greenberg.

*Science. 166:851. N. 14, '69. Environmental studies: OST [Office of Science and Technology] report urges better effort. L. J. Carter.

Science. 166:1487-91. D. 19, '69. Conservation law I: seeking a breakthrough in the courts. L. J. Carter.

Technology Review. 72:27-35. O.-N. '69. Modification of planet earth by man. G. J. F. MacDonald.

Technology Review. 72:33-5. Ja. '70. Oil spills: the need for law and science. J. A. Fay.

Texas Quarterly. 11:11-154. Summer '68. Limitations of the earth —a compelling focus for geology.

Time: 94:38+. Ag. 15, '69. Ecology: the new Jeremiahs.

Times (London). p 8. O. 7, '69. Man's deteriorating environment. Sir Julian Huxley and Max Nicholson.

*Trial. 5:53-4. F.-Mr. '69. A jet-age health hazard. W. H. Stewart.

*Trial. 5:10-11. Ag.-S. '69. Can law reclaim man's environment? R. S. Jacobson.

U.S. News & World Report. 68:5. F. 2, '70. Latest moves on pollution control.

UNESCO Courier. 22:4-40. Ja. '69. Can we keep our planet habitable?

UNESCO Courier. 22:6-9. Ag.-S. '69. Saving our vanishing forests. K. H. Oedekoven.

UNESCO Courier. 22:33-5. Ag.-S. '69. The pollution of the ocean. Nicolai Gorsky.

United States Naval Institute Proceedings. 95:63-75. My. '69. Oil pollution, no solution? T. A. Clingan, Jr.

University: A Princeton Quarterly. p 3-12. Winter '69-'70. The battle over America's environment. T. C. Southerland, Jr.

Wall Street Journal. p 6. Ag. 28, '69. Pollution: are nuclear reactors safe? N. L. Clemons.

Wall Street Journal. p 22. N. 26, '69. Conservation gains political weight. J. E. Bylin.

Wall Street Journal. p 24. D. 2, '69. Ecology & problems beyond pollution. Lee Berton.

Wall Street Journal. p 1+. D. 18, '69. Hudson river cleanup turns out to be slow and frustrating task. John Barnett.

Wall Street Journal. p 1+. D. 31, '69. Changing climate. R. D. James.

Wall Street Journal. p 1+. Ja. 6, '70. Embattled corps. Tom Herman.

Wall Street Journal. p 10. Ja. 8, '70. Air pollution: the big problem is you. S. MacDonald.

Washington Post. p D 1+. O. 5, '69. This lovely land of ours is plagued by ugly sores. Charlton Ogburn, Jr.

*Washington Post. p B 1+. O. 19, '69. Public fights A-power. Victor Cohn.

*Washington Post. p L 11. N. 8, '69. Taxation urged to help prevent further pollution. I. R. Barnes.